If I Make a Million
She'll Not Get a Penny

If I Make a Million
She'll Not Get a Penny

By
Norla Rankin

ISBN-13 978-0-9710929-8-3

Library of Congress Control Number: 2011943920

Printed in the United States of America
Set in Adobe Garamond Pro

This story has not been written by the person concerned,
but by someone who was fully aware of all the facts at the time.

Contents

PREFACE

In 1990, while I was on holiday in Cornwall, I needed a book to read—something easy that I could pick up and put down and not lose the jist of the story.

My usual favorites were light detective stories, but biographies seemed a better choice for my holiday reading.

I was struck by the title *The Richest Man in the World—the Sultan of Brunei* by James Bartholomew.

I had vaguely heard of the Sultan of Brunei but knew nothing about him.

I went into the shop and enquired from the assistant what the book was like.

"It's different," she said, "but worth reading, it's nice to know how the rich live—that's if you want to of course."

I bought it, but complained all the way back to the hotel about how much I had to pay for the paperback.

Back at my hotel, reading through the preface, I was surprised to learn that the Sultan of Brunei had not wanted this book to appear.

So many people will either say very little or nothing at all. Even the most willing sources have to calculate whether a particular piece of information can be traced back to them.

They decline to speak on the telephone from Brunei, (It is widely believed that the equivalent of the Special Branch, monitors international calls).

In such circumstances, facts are not easily won, and are often difficult to confirm.

None the less, I have researched this book exhaustively and am satisfied that all the facts in it are accurate.

The publishers of the book had apparently been contacted on the Sultan's behalf by a firm of solicitors saying, "His Majesty has in the past and continues in the present to protect his privacy and his reputation." They added, "He has not authorized Mr. Bartholomew [sic] in any such endeavor." The preface read:

> The Sultan is the absolute ruler of a nation of some 400,000 people. His powerful public role removes, in my view, any right he might otherwise have to privacy. But his power and massive wealth make his desire for privacy a considerable obstacle to research. Those close to the Sultan, know that if they are discovered talking to the media about him, they will be in trouble. They depend on him for their livelihood. Expatriates in Brunei also need him for the success of their businesses. Some companies working for the Sultan have a secrecy clause written into their contracts.
>
> No one wants to be quoted. One interviewee, a former member of the S.A.S. threatened my life if I named him in the book. More temperate souls told me at the outset of the interviews that every thing they said must be unattributable and in fact I have attributed almost nothing. I have wanted to protect all those people who had sufficient trust in me to tell me a part of what they know. To all these sources, unnamed for their own sakes I say a heartfelt thank you.
>
> James Bartholomew

Having read the preface, I felt encouraged to continue with the rest of the book. It proved interesting holiday reading, although sometimes I found some of the things hard to believe. That one man could have so much total power I could not understand.

I had been told at various times during my life that "money means power."

If I did not realize then that, by a strange quirk of fate, almost five years later I was to find out to my cost, just how true that was.

Chapter 1

Today is the 24th of August. I had always remembered it because it was my father's birthday. Now I remember it for a very different reason.

It was on this day nine years ago, in 1986 that I foolishly did something that I was to regret for many years. Looking back it is easy to ask why.

During this time I have had many critics and few supporters, and loyalty has been confined to the few from whom I would not have expected it.

The previous day my husband and I had been visiting my grandson, who was ill, when his father, Ivica, said to us, "I have a money problem."

"Haven't we all," I answered.

"Yes, but this is different. It is only a temporary short term cash flow crisis."

"I understand and wish that I could help you, but there seems to be no way that I can."

Ivica continued, "The trouble is that the hotel needs further investment and, at the same time, the builders want to be paid for the work that they have already done. We need £75,000. My two partners have been able to get their share, and now it is up to me to get the rest—otherwise, we could lose the hotel."

"I'm so sorry and really wish that I could help. How long would you need the money for?"

"Three months at the most—probably until Christmas."

I went home and thought about it for a long time (but obviously not long enough). There was one way that I could help.

The next day, I put forward a proposition to Ivica. He had convinced me that his explanation of the situation was the truth. But then I had no reason to disbelieve him.

"Ivica, I have been thinking—there may be a way that I can help you. I have a cottage which was left to me by my parents as security for my old age.

It is rented but I am prepared to let you have the deeds as collateral for a bank loan, but remember it is only for about the three months that you said you will need it."

Ivica appeared very surprised, gave me a hug and said, "I can't believe that you would do this for me. It seems that you are the only friend that I have at the moment, and I will never forget you for it, and remember that you will be welcome at the hotel any time. There will always be a meal available for you."

The next day, having collected the deeds of the cottage, Ivica and I went to the bank and were ushered graciously into the manager's office. I realized at once that the two were on very friendly terms. The usual formalities over, the manager put a folder of papers on the desk, with only the last sheet visible.

"I understand that you are acting as a short term guarantor for Ivica for £25,000 until Christmas. Is that right?"

Before I could answer, he said, "Will you just sign here," pointing at the last page.

"That is all you have to do, there is no need for you to read the document. It is quite irrelevant and would take you too long."

That was my first big mistake, but at that time I did not know that the father of my grandchild was a gambler, a womanizer, and, at my expense, was to find out later that he was also an inveterate liar.

The first surprise I had was to learn within seven weeks of the meeting in the bank, that the hotel, which I was told would be saved, went into voluntary liquidation.

No money was available for me from this liquidation, so I registered as a creditor. I should have realized that my money had not been used to save the business, so now I had to find out what the money had been used for.

Ivica was still insisting that it had been used for the purpose of trying to save the hotel despite the fact that there was written proof that it had not.

This was to be the beginning of a seven year battle, involving newspapers, High Commissions, The Home Office, private investigators, bailiffs, the courts, and most sections of the law.

Shortly afterwards, the liquidators sold the hotel for an unrealistically low price, to a friend of the three partners.

This "friend," when it was suggested to him that he should resell the property at a higher price, so that the creditors could recoup at least some of their money, replied by saying, "Make me do that and I will stand up in court and say that the money was to cover gambling debts that the three incurred in my casino during the last few years."

"Can you prove it?" asked the man acting for the liquidators.

"I won't have to. It's you lot who'll have to come forward with all the proof. Now get out of my office"

The man acting for the liquidators was an ex-policeman and had dealings with this person many times before, and knew that there was nothing that he could do.

The funds that had been allocated for this case had run out, and none of the creditors were prepared to spend any more of their money pursuing him privately.

"Of course," the ex-policeman said, "you could always do it yourself."

"I am not even a creditor of the hotel, and in any case I have no money to waste. They are all too clever for me and for the law so it seems," said the new owner.

Within a couple of months, Ivica and his friend decided on another venture. Again with borrowed money, they bought a pub, and with their usual enthusiasm went about renovating and completely refurbishing it.

"It will be worth it in the end. Leave it as it is and we will not make any money. This way we stand to make a lot," Ivica told me.

I had heard this sort of thing several times before.

I replied, "So what about my money? I don't need it at the moment, but don't forget that I have to have it before I am 65."

He smiled at me and said, "You'll have your money long before that, I promise."

That was my second mistake—believing him.

My cottage had been let to a tenant and to his family before him for many years. Quite unexpectedly, although now being an old man, the tenant decided to move.

Now I had the chance to sell and have money for my old age.

I telephoned Ivica and explained the situation to him saying, "I have to sell, but if you still need a couple of thousand for a little longer, I will give you the money when I have it from the sale. But I need the deeds and want you to come to the bank with me tomorrow." I had assumed that Ivica had been regularly paying off some of the debt.

"Yes that will be fine," he said, "what time shall I meet you there?"

"It will have to be in the morning, we can arrange a time later."

I was waiting for a call from him the next morning so I was surprised to hear my daughter's voice saying, "Mum, I'll have to come to the bank with you—Ivica is not here."

"What do you mean, not there?"

"He's gone."

"Gone where?"

"I have no idea."

"When did he leave, I was speaking to him last night?"

"I know, but Ivica had gone when I woke up."

"Where is Alexander?"

"With me and he is fine, I'll meet you in the bank at 11 o'clock."

I found it difficult to understand what my daughter was telling me, but as she did not seem worried, I decided that I would meet her at the bank as arranged. I could not believe that Ivica would abandon my daughter and his son without any warning, but I soon learned that he had.

4

Ivica had given me the understanding that he had been making regular repayments to the bank, and that the initial loan was now much less.

I met my daughter, Trudy, at the bank. This time we were not greeted as cordially as before. We were shown into the manager's office, but I was surprised to find that the man with whom I had dealt with before was not there.

"Good morning," I said.

"My name is Mr. Sterling. Mr. Hendon is no longer at this branch."

"Then where can I see him?"

"I'm sorry you can't; he has been moved to London and is no longer dealing with this matter—you will have to deal with me."

"With all due respect you cannot be aware of the personal arrangement that I had with the bank regarding the loan to Ivica."

"I certainly am. It was a straightforward mortgage on your cottage."

"I was told absolutely nothing about this. All I agreed to do was to be guarantor for the £25,000 short-term loan for Ivica."

"But you signed this form Mrs. McBride, I have a copy here."

He passed the paper over to me, and I agreed that I had signed, but said that I was not at any time told that it was for a mortgage to be taken out against my property.

Mr. Sterling replied, "You are an intelligent woman. What did you think you were signing?"

"I have just told you that I thought that it was a private agreement between Ivica and me. I was told not to waste my time reading the contents, because they were totally irrelevant, and would take too long."

"Well I am sorry but this is the situation and there is nothing that can be done about it."

I was not prepared for this confrontation, but did my best not to show how intimidated I really felt.

"So tell me the worst. I understand that Ivica has been making regular payments for the past twelve months, so the debt must be considerably reduced by now. I have repeatedly asked the bank for statements, but they have refused to send them to me, saying that as the account is not in my name I have no right to know."

"Yes, that is the policy of the bank. The amount owing now stands at £33,000," answered Mr. Sterling.

This was too much for me. I couldn't believe what he was saying, and could hardly get any coherent words out. Eventually I said, "How can that possibly be?"

"Mr. Kalebic was unable to make any repayments, and asked the manager for a further £7,000 overdraft."

"Without my permission, you must be joking!"

"I assure you that I am not, Mrs. McBride, and I assume that you are not responsible, since you were not here with Ivica at the time he asked for a further overdraft."

"Exactly," I said.

Mr. Sterling asked, "Did no-one tell you about it?"

Without waiting for my answer, he went on to explain complicated banking laws of which I was totally ignorant. This seemed to be for his benefit more than for mine, and then he said, "You have a choice, you either pay us the money owed now or incur interest for every day that you default."

In disbelief, I said, "So is that it?"

"I'm afraid so. It's up to you to decide what you want to do. If you don't have the money available, you will have to sell the cottage very quickly, otherwise we will have foreclose on the cottage. You must realize that the longer you leave it the more you will have to pay," said Mr. Sterling.

I left the bank with my daughter confused and upset. I found it hard to believe that this could happen. Why should I have to pay off somebody else's debt?

I had been conned into this predicament, so now I was determined to try to do something about it.

I tried to contact Ivica, but without success.

"I understand that he is playing poker in Malta," a friend of Ivica's told me when I telephoned him. "He usually disappears when he can't face a problem"

Nobody I spoke to could or would tell me how I could get in touch with Ivica, and I had no time to waste. The bank had given me an ultimatum.

Chapter 2

I was lucky to sell the cottage fairly soon, but at a much lower price than its market value. Fortunately, it was enough to pay off the debt, and by that Christmas I decided that I would no longer just get angry—I would try to get EVEN.

Ivica was a comparatively young man. I was getting old. We moved in completely different circles, but he was the father of my grandson, and I at least owed something to that four year old. Now I had a little more confidence and calculated what I could do.

Seeking legal advice was the obvious thing, and at that time I had faith in the legal system. I had no reason to doubt that this was the best thing to do.

Seven years later I was to find out that it was not.

During my visit to the solicitor who was going to take up my case, he said to me, "But, Mrs. McBride, you have no proof that the money owing to the bank was not your own debt. There is nothing in writing that shows otherwise."

"The bank knows, surely."

"Maybe, but there is nothing in writing, and the only signature that they have is yours."

"Yes I understand, you are quite right."

How could I have been so stupid!

The first thing I had to do now was to find Ivica. I knew that he was adept at avoiding difficult situations—and this was certainly one of these. But I had to try.

I spent the next few months trying to trace him in my own country and others. I telephoned as far afield as America, Hong Kong, Malaysia, and Yugoslavia with no result. But, about a year later, luck must have been on my side for once. I was able to speak to him for the first time since we had met at the bank to sign for the loan. Ivica eventually agreed to meet me with my daughter, Trudy, at a hotel near my home.

Ivica greeted us as if nothing had happened.

"How nice it is to see you again! I should not have left like I did. I only wish I could turn the clock back. How is Alexander? I have missed him so much. Please, try not to blame too much."

I knew that if I let myself feel sorry for him, all would be lost. Although since I am a sensitive person, I wondered whether this time he was being sincere. Ivica was not.

It took four hours for Ivica to sign a document saying that he owed me the money.

Ivica was later to stand up in court and say that this had been done under duress.

A 65 year old female pensioner against a 38 year old strong man—what nonsense! Maybe the judge believed him; Ivica was very convincing as always.

We decided to have more coffee before we left the hotel.

Having thanked the waitress for being a witness to his signature. Just before leaving, Ivica told us that he was desperately unhappy, shed a few tears and said again that he should never have left.

Lying came so very easily to him, but now I felt a little relieved, thinking that from now on things would be simple and straightforward.

With the proof that I had, I thought the law would be able to help me.

How wrong I was!

At least now I could go to the bank and get them to admit that I was misinformed about the loan to Ivica, and had not been asked about a further advancement that had been given to him without my permission. This was surely illegal.

Eventually, after a great deal of wrangling, I received a payment of £5,000 as what was called a "kind gesture" by the bank, which, at the same time, admitted no liability whatsoever.

Later, I learned that had I pursued the matter through the courts I could well have received the full amount. On the other hand, had I lost, I would have had to pay very high costs to the bank and to the courts. I now had very little money left and could not afford the risk. I literally had no choice.

I still had no idea what had been done with my money, but one day several months later when I was speaking to a friend, she said, "I was so sorry to hear about your problem. Alexander must miss his father. Does he see him?"

"Not often, but I wouldn't know very much about that."

"Is Ivica living with his new girlfriend?"

"Which one is that?"

"The one who's car he has been driving for the past year."

"Which, the red BMW, I thought that belonged to a colleague who had lost his license for drunk driving?" I said.

"If you believe that you will believe anything."

"But he used that car while he still lived at Farm Drive."

"I know, but his girlfriend used to pick him up every day, and then he had full use of the BMW whenever he needed it. Apparently she is some foreigner who is related to a very wealthy and influential family."

"He would probably say that to impress people, anyway where did you get all this information?" I asked.

"Everybody is talking about it."

"Why, what is the interest?"

"I think it is because he says that he has got himself a meal ticket for life, and that he is madly in love this time."

"He says that every time he leaves one woman and child for another," I answered.

"Apparently this time it is different. At least that is what he is saying."

Whatever car Ivica ever had, the number plate was always the same— YOGIIT. It was specialized and he was very proud of it. After some time he became known by its name. Towards the end of the relationship with my daughter he sold his car and did not intend buying a new one because as Ivica

11

told us, "There is no point really. A very good friend of mine has lost his license through drunk driving and will not be using his car for eighteen months at least, and he has told me that I can use it whenever I want to."

"That sounds reasonable," I replied, "and as Trudy has her own, there should be no problem."

"The problem I have is that I have no car to put my number plate on," answered Ivica.

I suggested, "Then sell it and get some money for it. You need it at the moment."

"I can't do that" he said. "It means too much to me. Can I ask you a favor?"

"As long as it is not to borrow any more money."

"Don't be silly," said Ivica with a disarming smile. "Do you think that your husband, Mac, could put it on your car for the time being?"

"I don't see why not as long as it doesn't cost us anything," I answered, cooperating.

So it was arranged and the number plate transferred through all the proper channels. We now had his specialized number plate on our car.

It caused no problem until our license was due for renewal. When we applied for the renewal at the Driver and Vehicle Licensing Agency, we were told that this was not our number plate!

It belonged to a BMW and they would not issue us with a new license until we replaced the number!

Apart from being shocked we were very annoyed, and assured the licensing department that we were the rightful owners of the plate.

Obviously, the person who owned the BMW had more authority regarding the license than we did, and despite all our efforts we were not able to find out, from the licensing department, to whom it belonged.

However, a man who was doing some enquiry work on our behalf at the time, was able to tell us that the number plate was now on the 'so called borrowed' car that Ivica had told us about. As always this was a pack of lies, and it belonged to a Mariam Isa, the wealthy girl that Ivica was to marry a few years later.

When I realized all the inconvenience that we would be caused by the license, I discovered that this Mariam Isa had a flat in Cardiff, and decided to pay her a visit.

Having no satisfaction from the visit, I wrote Mariam Isa a letter which read:

> Last night I called at your flat to discuss the matter of your cherished number plates, 'YOGIIT.' You were most impolite to me and did not even have the decency to come to your door—you even refused to have a civilized conversation with me through your intercom. I thought that as I was a 70 year old and you, little more than twenty, you would have shown a little more respect. Your bad manners upset me a lot, so now I feel that I must tell you the rest of the story, in case you do not know.
>
> The man from whom you had those plates is the father of my illegitimate grandson.
>
> He had been living with my daughter and his son for four years before he disappeared, leaving a debt of £30,000, which had to be paid by me. I want you to understand that he now owes me that amount of money with interest. I need to have his new address in this country and am sure that you have this. You must know that he has abandoned his son, and is at the moment out of the country.
>
> All that I have told you can be confirmed by my solicitor and the bank, the names of whom I will give to you.
>
> We knew your car well when it had the original number plates on it, as Ivica parked it often outside our cottage when he was with us.
>
> I would appreciate an early reply so that we may be able to resolve this problem with the licensing department. It would be so much easier than involving the police at this stage.

Needless to say, I did not receive a reply, and it became quite a complicated issue to sort out our car plates.

By now I realized that she had no more principles than Ivica. They both had a complete disregard for the feelings and sensibilities of others.

Having digressed back to what the friend had told me about Ivica's new love, in retrospect it was obvious where my money had gone.

He had spent it on this girl, who was younger than one of his two daughters (the one who was a Page Three girl),[1] to try to impress her, if he was able to do this, he could see his chance of a wonderful life and lifestyle ahead.

This was a chance that he could not afford to miss. Ivica was a gambler and this was a gamble well worth taking despite all the heartbreak he would cause other people.

---

[1] A Page Three girl is a model for topless photographs published in UK tabloids, usually on page three of The Sun and The Daily Star.

Chapter 3

Now, knowing this, I was more determined than ever to get even with him.

When next I saw my solicitor he said to me, "Right, now we can take him to court to try to get a judgment against him."

"What do you think our chances are?"

"With all the information that we have, that part should be easy. But getting the money is a completely different matter. Shall we just go one step at a time, and see what happens? It will probably be an endless battle, but if you feel it is worth the worry and, might I say, money, then we can go straight ahead."

"What are my chances of getting legal aid?"

"Pretty poor, I imagine, but we can try."

It was many months later before we had a hearing in court. Ivica, when asked by the judge how he intended to pay his debt, said that when he left, he deposited the shares that he had in the new pub with his accountant, and had asked that they be put into the name of my daughter, Trudy, so that I could be paid from that source.

Unfortunately all files relating to this transaction were conveniently mislaid by the firm of solicitors acting for Ivica—the share certificates too!

The police, who were informed, investigated this firm for fraud, (at least that is what I was told) with no positive result. Every thing was soon forgotten, but not by me.

There seemed little else that I could do at the moment. The judge had said after the hearing, "We have to work within the law Mrs. McBride."

"But he is not telling the truth," I protested.

"Maybe not, but you have to prove that he is lying. He does not have to prove that he is telling the truth. You can of course pursue it, but it could cost you a lot of money, plus his costs if you lose."

"Thank you, I will have to think about what I will do next."

The law was on his side again, and he seemed to know exactly how to use it for his benefit.

Then quite unexpectedly Ivica applied to the courts for access to his son, my grandson. A date was fixed for the hearing. So now I knew where he would be on that day.

After much discussion with my solicitor, he agreed that he should be able to serve Ivica with a writ as he came out of the court. My husband and I decided to wait in the reception hall on the day of the hearing. We were, of course, most concerned to know the outcome of it, but at the same time did not want to miss this rare opportunity of confronting him.

The waiting seemed endless.

Eventually the solicitor came up to us and said, rather impatiently, "I think he must have gone out another way."

"There is no other way!"

"Well surely he can't still be in there. I shall have to go very soon. I have other work to do and hope you realize that you will have to pay me for my time."

He need not have told me this as I had learned over the years that it was I who had to pay for everything, despite the fact that it was I, who was the injured party.

"Can't somebody else serve him with the writ—an interested party or relation?"

My solicitor responded, "I don't really know. Ah—there's a colleague; he's a barrister, maybe he will know."

"John, tell me, what is the position about serving a writ? Can a friend or relation do it?"

John answered, "Sorry old chap, it's out of my field. Haven't a clue, maybe someone else can help."

This did nothing to bolster my confidence in the legal system.

Then we got lucky. Ivica came down into the reception hall while we were still there, and we duly served him with the writ.

His surprise was obvious as he walked away arm-in-arm with his new girlfriend.

He had come to get access to his son, but that was not all that he got!

The solicitor acting for him had been informed by letter of the outstanding debt, but had not had the courtesy to reply. Ivica continued to see his son at monthly intervals. The judge had stipulated that his visits would have to be on a regular basis. If he did not turn up as arranged, he would not see Alexander until the next month.

As was expected, Ivica was unable to keep to this routine for very long. He always had excuses. Either the plane was late, or he had a business meeting out of the country.

For the child's sake he was allowed a little compromise in these circumstances, but, predictably, he took advantage of the situation.

I had many telephone conversations with Ivica at that time, most of them the same.

Ivica called to say, "Hello, I'm ringing to ask if you will arrange for me to see Alexander. I'm missing him so very much and Trudy doesn't seem to understand."

I replied, "I'm not surprised after the way you have treated them both. Anyway why are you asking me? You have made no effort to pay me any of the money that you owe me, nor have you contributed a penny towards the little fellow, your son. Do you honestly expect me to do anything to help you?"

"I know it's a lot to ask, but I have no money," moaned Ivica.

"Ivica, don't tell me that it is beyond your capability to get at least a couple of thousand to ease my situation."

"Believe me I really can't."

"Believe you—you must be joking! I'm sure it would be a different story if you wanted money to spend on any of your lady friends, or if you wanted to go to the casino. You've already conned me out of £30,000. The best thing that you can do is sell some of your expensive jewellery."

"I can't do that; it all has sentimental value."

"So what—I have had to sell some of mine to pay bills caused by you. Do you think that mine did not have any sentimental value? Another thing—how can you possibly afford continental holidays? I'd be happy with a week in Cornwall. By the way did that girl go with you?"

"Yes, but that is none of your business."

"That is where you are wrong. Just listen to me for one minute Ivica. As long as you owe me that amount of money, and make no contribution towards your son, then I will make it my business. Do you understand what I am saying?"

Sometimes, it was difficult to know whether he did or not, because although he spoke very good English, at times he did not seem to fully comprehend the meaning.

This had proved very useful for him. He was a very good actor, and had plenty of practice.

"I do not intend to stand by and watch you wine and dine that girl on my money!"

"What do you mean?" he spluttered, "I told you I lost that money."

"Tough, I don't give a damn what you say you did with it, because I just don't believe you. All you do is lie, lie, lie."

I took a deep breath, and tried to think more rationally—it was not easy.

"Let us talk about Alexander. Last time he had been with you and you took him back home, you left without telling the child how he could contact you if he wanted to. So what do you expect a five year old to think of a father who does that?"

"I don't have to tell anyone where I am, I've got a life of my own to lead. What do you want me to do-live like a monk?"

I felt that I couldn't continue this conversation. I was very upset and not getting anywhere, so all I said was, "When you have paid your debts and taken a little responsibility for your son, you can live any sort of life that you want to, but until then don't expect any favors from me."

I put the phone down but it rang again within a few minutes, and as if we had not had any of our previous conversation, he said to me, "You'll arrange it for me. I'll pick him up at 10 o'clock on Saturday morning. Tell Trudy."

I did, for the child's sake. They spent five hours together. Where, I do not know.

Sometimes, he would take his son to friends, sometimes to the casino where the little boy would play the machines, while his father was gambling at the poker table. Other times, they would spend with his Asian girlfriend.

When next I spoke to him I said, "Next time you have Alexander, please don't take him to your girlfriend's. She is always very rude to me when I ask for you, and I do not want my grandchild to be with her or her family, she might have a lot of money but she has no manners."

"That's blackmail," he said, "you can't tell me where I can and cannot take my own son—it's blackmail."

This time he screamed the words at me!

"Call it what you like. When I no longer have any sort of responsibility for him, and you are helping to support him, then you can call the tune. Until then, if you continue to lie, and think of no one but yourself, then I will make the rules. In future, when I ring, please ask your girlfriend to be polite to me."

I continued, "Incidentally Ivica, you know what you have to do to get me off your back. Think hard about it, as you should know by now that I really mean what I say."

Eventually he was told that the child no longer wanted to see him, as he was always so disappointed when his father did not turn up.

Ivica accepted this new arrangement.

Whilst he was still in a position to see the child he sent postcards and occasional presents to him. This stopped abruptly, and he neither saw nor contacted Alexander—not even on his birthday or at Christmas.

"Don't get mad—get even still haunted me." I was doing all I could and still getting nowhere.

And yet, I still spent time and money, at least any that I could still muster, so that eventually I would know that I had tried everything to recoup my badly needed funds.

This was proving to be much harder and to take much longer than I had anticipated.

Ivica had come to this country, reputedly as a refugee, with little money and nothing else except one asset—his plausibility. Some might call it the charm of a con man—the ladies at least. His first job was menial, so he became an inveterate gambler to supplement his income. Most of his gambling paid off. Now, I had to work on the assumption that one day Ivica's luck would run out.

After he had been in this country for a short while, he married an English girl and had two children. He opened a club and restaurant, financed of course on borrowed money.

Borrow, gamble, and con the gullible, that was his adage.

At this point, I can make no excuse for what I did.

At my age I should have known better, but then we all know that it is easy to be wise after the event.

Within a few years of his marriage, Ivica had set up home with another woman, and they had children.

For the next eight years he had two family homes. His wife was never aware of this, which proves how clever he has always been.

His businesses were now developing problems. The children's private education had to be paid for—oh yes, he had high aspirations for them all, and his gambling and womanizing had to be funded. He had for many years been robbing Peter to pay Paul, but now there seemed to be no way out.

Then a colleague suggested for Ivica to become a third partner in a hotel project. The three would invest an equal amount to purchase the hotel.

A large grant would be available, as the property had been badly neglected over the years.

With a substantial loan from the bank they set about renovating it and it seemed to be turning into a great success, but it didn't, and that is where my story began.

Having received no payment from him for a long time, I was surprised when I received a phone call from a friend in 1990 saying, "You are not going to believe this. I've just been speaking to Susan, and she said that they have just had an invitation to a very posh wedding in Brunei."

"Who is getting married?" I asked.

"Ivica. Apparently the girl is besotted with him, and it's to be a lavish affair. She told me that many of his affluent friends are being invited—so that leaves you and me out! And their flights are being paid for, so I understand."

When next I heard from the same friend it was to tell me that the wedding had taken place.

"Can you believe it?" my friend said, "3,000 guests with the service being broadcast outside the church for those who were unable to get in."

"I thought he was still married to Pat."

"He says he got a quickie divorce in Yugoslavia, you know, where he was born."

"It must have been vastly different from his first wedding," I said.

"Yes, and I understand that Ivica had to change his religion for the family to accept him. But I suppose that is a small price to have to pay for the life of luxury that he'll now have at their expense. I wonder how long this marriage will last."

"As long as the money lasts I suppose, because I can't honestly see him changing his ways," I said.

"Neither can I, but he dare not start womanizing and gambling. He has got too much to lose if he is found out. But then he is a clever individual, and, so far, avoided being found out."

"I agree, but he is dealing with very influential people now, and if they do not like what he is doing he could well be gotten rid of," I said.

"Anyway I thought you would like to know the latest. If I hear anything else I'll let you know."

"Thanks a lot, speak to you soon."

I came away from the telephone more determined than ever to try to get my money back. He surely had access to money and would pay off his debt to me. I was wrong to even think it. He was far too busy calculating his own future, to give it, or to his son.

Eventually, after a lot of hard work and worry, I took Ivica to court again in 1994 and was awarded a High Court Judgment against him for the money that he owed me. The judge told him that the amount would incur interest at the usual rate until the money was paid.

When eventually the legal system was able to get him to court again, in between his world-wide travels, in answer to some of the judge's questions, he said, "Your honor, I have as you say a very expensive lifestyle, but all this, I do assure you, is paid for by my wife's family."

"Do you not have any money of your own Mr. Kalebic?"

"No sir, I don't really need it. My house is paid for, so are all the expenses, plus air fares and all entertainment. I also have a gold card to shop for clothes and personal things anywhere I wish."

"You seem to be a very lucky man Mr. Kalebic, but how do you intend to pay off this debt?"

"Well—as I'm sure you will understand, I would like to have a little independence, so a friend and I are hoping to open a restaurant in London very soon. Once that is established, I hope to be able to repay this debt. I have always said, that when I have the money, I will pay the lady."

"Well I sincerely hope that you will, but remember that the longer you leave it the more you will have to pay."

Those were the glib answers that Ivica had given in the court room. But what I was told that he said in an anti-room a few minutes later and in the presence of my solicitor and colleagues was a different story.

I shall remember for a very long time. It was, "IF I MAKE A MILLION SHE WILL NOT GET A PENNY."

Chapter 4

Now that Ivica was back in London, he could be followed more easily. So I employed a private investigator, named Frank, who assured me that he could help, and at least get me some of the money that I was owed. He had known Ivica when they were both working in Cardiff.

They had been business and gambling friends although working in different fields. Frank seemed very optimistic and I had to pay a substantial amount to cover the cost of the initial plan of action, but I really believed that this time it would work.

"I've got it all arranged," Frank said, "I've found out that Ivica's car is permanently parked in the driveway of his very expensive house—you know about that don't you?"

"Yes, everybody seems to know about it."

"Right, then this is what we propose to do. The men who are helping me will go in with me, lift the car, take it some place where it will never be found, and you will get the money, less our cut."

"Surely that is illegal?"

"Not the way that we intend to do it. Anyway he'll never know who took it, and remember you know nothing about it"

"I don't really like it Frank, but as you say, he owes me money, and you are only using his methods of collecting debts. Didn't you say that you have done similar work for Ivica in the past?"

"That's right, but now he owes me, so I'm getting back at him this way."

This plan did not materialize.

However Frank assured me that it was only a temporary hitch. It was obviously not apparent to me at this time, that Ivica had all the support of his new family's money, legal advisors, and many top people of influence.

I found it hard to understand why my efforts to get back the money owing to me, would cause such concern to so many people. After all this amount of money was enormous to me, but to the likes of them surely not worth talking about.

Many of their family and friends would gamble that amount of money in one evening and even afford to lose it.

Apparently, one day when Frank was following Ivica, he waited in the car outside his house, and when Ivica finally passed, Frank wound down his window and said, "Hi, Yogiit."

Ivica turned and looked and then said, "Why are you still following me, can't you just leave me alone?"

"No I can't, I've come to collect for Mrs. McBride. It's long overdue."

Then Ivica repeated over and over again, "How many times have I got to tell everybody that I have no money."

And then, as if from nowhere, a tall well dressed man came up behind Ivica and frog-marched him away from the car and up to his front door.

As they walked away the tall well dressed man turned to Frank and said, "Bye, Frank, I don't want to see you hanging around here again."

"Tough luck, because you will, until the man you've just shoved through the front door pays the £30,000 he owes to my client. Tell him that from me will you?"

Obviously, now getting embarrassed, because the neighbors were aware of what was going on, the man quickly disappeared out of sight and slammed the front door.

I did not hear from Frank for a long time after that incident.

It was unusual, because he had in the past kept in regular touch. I tried contacting Frank on his various numbers with no luck.

Eventually Frank rang and said, "I have heard that Ivica will be in Cardiff on Friday. He's coming for the big fight. I didn't know he was that interested, but apparently his daughter, Anna-Maria, is one of the 'glamour girls' displaying the number of each round."

"I'm surprised that she would want to do that."

I replied, "Anything for publicity I suppose—not that she needs it having been a Page Three Girl for the past four years. Ivica is using the excuse that he doesn't get to see her often these days as he is out of the country so much. Anyway I will try to get down myself, because I'm sure that after the fight he will be in his usual haunt, the casino. He'll probably want to gamble his winnings or try to recoup his losses, knowing him!"

Things could go well this time. But I had been disappointed so many times before that I was now never optimistic. After the fight, he did go to the casino with plenty of cash as usual. Now the private investigator with the full authority of the courts could demand all that he had on him.

Frank approached Ivica and said, "This time Ivica, I won't take no for an answer. I know that you have a lot of cash on you at the moment, so I've come to collect. You know for whom."

What Ivica said to Frank I'm sure was unrepeatable but I understand that the main jist of the reply was, "Can't you see I'm playing for big stakes. See me later when you have made an appointment. That is what you have to do now—it's not like the old days."

"What the hell do you mean? We go back a long way and nothing's changed."

"That is where you are wrong, Frank, everything has changed, and don't you forget it."

"Say what you like, I will see you when you have finished your game. I am not on my own this time and you know my friends very well from the past. They are apt to lose patience much quicker than I. See you soon."

When he went to meet him after the game, Frank was told that he had left, in a great hurry.

Frank telephoned me the next day from London to say how sorry he was that he was unable to get any money for me.

"What happened," I said, "I thought that everything was organized?"

"So did I, believe me Lorna, he just disappeared."

"What do you mean disappeared?"

"When I went back to the casino to look for him after his poker game, they said that Ivica had not been playing, and that he had left the building straight after he had spoken to me.

"I haven't any idea where he went because I spent half of the night, going to all the likely places where he might be.

"I even called on his sister, and got her out of bed, but she insisted that she had not seen him, but then you know as well as I do that she is as big a liar as he is."

At the time I was very surprised to know that Frank had not pursued Ivica further.

After all, they were both living in London at the same time for several months after their visit to Cardiff.

Normally, I would hear from Frank several times a week, but suddenly there was no contact from him at all. I often wonder whether he was encouraged to change sides. I have not been able to think of another reason for his sudden lack of communication. Maybe he realized that he would never be able to get my money for me, so he accepted a payoff from Ivica. After all money is a great temptation.

For the previous six months, The Sun newspaper had shown great interest in writing the story and I have to admit that Frank had worked very hard on my behalf to come to an agreement with them. Also, I was given to understand that all but the final details had been settled. However, out of the blue the telephone rang and when I picked up the receiver a voice at the other end said, "Hello Lorna, Wayne here, how are you these days?"

"Getting older and you? It's nice to hear from you, anyway how's the story going?"

"Well that is what I rang you about. I really don't know how to tell you this, but I heard from the editor today, and he said that he is no longer interested in writing your story. I am really so sorry."

"I'm sure it's not your fault but can you tell me why?"

"He wouldn't give a reason. I tried for you, but he just said no, that's it. As you know, we've been working on it for months. The only thing I've heard in the grapevine is that it has been blocked by somebody influential. Make what you wish of that, but I'm sure that you have a damn good idea who that might be."

Yet again money and influence seemed to have come to the fore and apparently I was not entitled to any explanation.

In the meanwhile, the Court Bailiffs had gone into Ivica's home to claim anything that was his.

There was just £750 worth of items—hard to believe in a house worth £1,500,000, but I thought at least this would pay my court fees.

But that was not to be. Solicitors acting for his father-in-law, Pehin Isa,[2] wrote to me saying that if any item was removed from the house they would take the matter further. They could sue me, and they had ample money to do that.

I decided that it was not worth pursuing this for such a small amount, knowing that in the end I would be throwing good money after bad.

At least the judge had awarded me costs of about £350, and I thought I would be paid that soon. This was not the case because I was informed by letter a few weeks later that I would not get the money, as Ivica had received legal aid for the hearing.

---

[2] Pehin Isa served as the Special Adviser to His Majesty the Sultan of Brunei as well as the Minister of Home Affairs until 24th May 2005.

Chapter 5

By now I was being advised by friends, family, and even solicitors, and all who had known him in the past, to stop pursuing Ivica for my money.

They said, "Count your losses and forget him. You are only making yourself ill with all the worry, and the sod has no intention of paying you a penny. Think, with all the influence and money he has through his new connections, he will always be one step ahead of you. Apparently his wife is still besotted with him, and as long as she is happy, her family is going to protect him."

I couldn't take their advice.

Fortunately, I still had a few good friends who were prepared to help me, and pass on any new information that they might have about his travels and businesses. It seemed such a long time until I finally heard from one who told me, "Have you heard the latest news about Ivica? I don't know whether it is true or not, but somehow I think that it must be."

"I've not heard anything, is it good or bad?" I asked.

"Well I don't know really, but Ivica has opened a restaurant with an Italian friend, in the basement of a London hotel. If that is the case he will surely have some assets that you can get at."

"It's something to work on at least, if it is true. I'll contact my solicitor straight away to see if there is anything that we can do—at least we know where he is at the moment, but for how long I wonder?"

On this information, my solicitor suggested that I should apply to the courts again, and serve him with a writ to attend an oral examination.

This was obtained very quickly, but, as always, he had some excuse for not being able to attend the first hearing. His reasons were long and numerous, but eventually some weeks later he did attend the hearing.

It was several months later that I received a transcript of the hearing. There had as always been complications even on that occasion. The County Court in West Kensington had not been able to deal with the case, because there was no district judge available, despite the fact that they had been given at least one month's notice of the hearing.

Fortunately, it was transferred to another court some distance away, where the examination took approximately three hours.

Ivica stood in court and answered all questions without hesitation. He had no solicitor with him, and soon convinced the judge that he had no money with which to pay his debt—no sources of income, no savings, no bank, building society or Post Office accounts.

When asked whether at any time he used any other name he answered, "No sir, never."

"I will repeat the question, are you sure that you never at any time use another name?"

"Definitely not—never."

That of course was a blatant lie, because he had told his son, Alexander, and others that he was to be called Adam from now on, as that was his Muslim name.

"Have you changed your religion?"

"No sir, I am still Catholic as I was born."

These were just two of many lies that he told under oath, but, as I have explained before, it would have cost me too much to pursue the matter.

During the examination, he also denied knowing anything about his father-in-law, Pehin Isa, except to say that he is someone in the Brunei government where his wife comes from.

Ivica insisted that this was all he knew, despite the fact that Pehin Isa's position was common knowledge.

"So where do you live?"

"At 55 Porchester Terrace."

Ivica was then asked to describe the type of house.

He replied, "It is large, has two reception rooms, and seven bedrooms."

"And how do you pay for this?"

"I don't, everything is paid for by a company."

"Will you tell us the name of this company?"

"I'm sorry, sir, I don't know."

"You mean to tell me that a company that you do not know the name of pays all expenses for you? Might I ask why they should do that?"

"I do not need to know, but obviously it has some connection with my father-in-law."

"But you just told me that you did not know anything about him. Do you wish to retract that statement?"

"No sir, I do not."

"How are you able to afford all these lavish trips and holidays abroad?"

"They are always paid for by the company or my wife's family."

"I think that you are a very fortunate man, Mr. Kalebic, and should make some effort to pay off your long standing debt to Mrs. McBride—I understand that you own an expensive watch, why do you not sell it and get some money?"

"I have already explained that I had to sell it when I needed some extra money urgently."

"What did you need that extra money for? You have already told me that everything is paid for, even clothes and entertainment. What more could you possibly want?"

Ivica hesitated for quite a while before saying, "It was for personal reasons, sir."

He was a gambler and could have incurred gambling debts with people who would not wait to be paid.

All I could do now was wait. The days seemed endless. It was difficult to concentrate on other things, but life had to go on.

Within a week my solicitor sent me a copy of authority from Ivica and the court, to make any necessary enquiries into his financial circumstances.

I was also advised that Ivica had completed and sworn his testimony on oath in an affidavit. The judge had apparently warned him about the consequences of any of the facts being found to be untrue.

He need not have bothered because no attention had been paid to all the lies that he had told under oath in the past.

One day when I was contemplating the whole sorry situation, I thought there must be something else I can do—but what? I suppose I could contact my local member of parliament, an "MP," as they were called. Yes, that's a good idea I thought, but no one seemed to agree with me on that.

"You are wasting your time," was the reaction that I got from everybody.

My answer was, "I have the time and as long as it doesn't cost me, what the hell have I got to lose?"

I went to one of the MP's surgeries, as they are called these days, and then another, and another, and another with little success.

In fairness I think that the MP tried, but came up against the same problem as everybody else. This family that Ivica had married into was so wealthy and influential, that nobody seemed to want to enquire into anything remotely connected with them.

Could it be political? I was really beginning to believe that it might be, but I could never really know.

During my last visit with my MP, I said, "I realize that it must be difficult for you, but could I ask if you could just get one small bit of information for me?"

"If I can, I certainly will; what is it you want to know?"

"His present nationality," I replied.

"Is that all?"

"Yes, thank you."

"Then, that should be no problem."

But, of course, I should have known that it was a problem and a big one.

Each time I received a letter headed The House of Commons, my hopes were raised only to be dashed once I had read the contents.

Surely, it had not been too much to ask, what the nationality of Ivica was. He had once been married to an English girl and had automatically become 'British,' and had a right to stay in this country.

He was divorced, and had married a foreign Muslim girl, but not an ordinary Muslim girl, but one with close connections to a very influential family and apparently had some sort of immunity.

The letter I received from the Home Office was polite but final. They would not tell me what I wanted to know because this man was entitled to his privacy. They also pointed out that they had no reason to believe that he was in the country illegally, although they had had no communication from him since 1973.

So that was it. Neither I nor the local MP could make any further enquiries.

In the meantime, I had received a letter from a solicitor whom I had not heard of before, making me an offer. He was offering, on behalf of one of his clients, to buy the judgment from me for a fixed sum. The sum was ridiculously low, and the conditions attached totally unreasonable. I had to refuse.

Sometime during those last few weeks I had read an interesting story in one of the national newspapers. It was about the purchase of a very prestigious car, by the Sultan of Brunei for whom Ivica's father-in-law, Pehin Isa, worked.

Whenever I heard or read things like this I became incensed.

I realize that the debt had nothing directly to do with this wealthy family, but at the same time, I felt that, to them, the amount owing to me was so little, and could easily be paid.

This particular newspaper as with many others were always asking for comments from readers, so I decided that I would write to them, and this is what I wrote:

Dear Sir,

Reading that some ideas for comments or interesting stories are welcome, might I suggest one, having read the article in your paper several days ago about the acquisition of a prestigious car by the Sultan of Brunei.

Whilst I agree that many of your readers would be interested in the profuse wealth of the man, might I suggest at the same time some might know that the son-in-law of his financial advisor, has an unpaid debt owing to a 70 year old pensioner, who has had a High Court Judgment against him for three years.

She has tried to recoup this £50,000 debt through official and legal sources without success.

It has been established in a London court, that the debtor is totally financed in his lavish lifestyle, by his father-in-law, so it is hard to credit that when public bailiffs attempted to recoup goods worth only a couple of hundred pounds, the financial advisor, through his solicitor informed the pensioner that action would be taken against her if she allowed them to proceed.

This was amazing reaction from a man who was working in high office for someone reputed to be worth about 22 billion pounds. Should you have any interest in this idea for a story, I can submit to you all legal court files, faxes from the relevant High Commission office, correspondence from the MP who was dealing with it on my behalf and anything else that might be of interest to you.

All this information is readily available.

I would greatly appreciate a reply from you.

Thanking you in anticipation.

Yours faithfully,

Of course, as I had come to expect, I received no reply. I suppose I had not really expected one but had hoped that they would have shown me that small courtesy.

By now, I had begun to believe that these people had influence everywhere and knew how and when to use it.

After all, it is said that money buys power.

Since I had been made an offer for the purchase of the judgment, I needed further clarification.

This, the solicitors acting on behalf of their unnamed client declined to give.

Without any more contact they withdrew their offer.

During the months following the oral examination, although Ivica was entertaining friends at his restaurant, and taking them to high class casinos and gambling establishments, no payment was ever made to me.

I kept on hoping that now he had a business, he would feel that he had to pay me something. But he did not.

Eventually I rang the restaurant and asked to speak to him. The man who answered said, "I'm sorry he is not here at the moment."

"When are you expecting him back?"

"I do not know; he left a message saying that he was going to Yugoslavia on holiday."

"When was that, and could you tell me who I am speaking to?"

"This is Pierro, his partner"

"I'm Lorna McBride, Trudy's mother. Do you have a telephone number where I can get hold of him?"

"I wish I could. I want to get hold of him urgently about this business. He seems to have disappeared, leaving me to settle a debt of £11,000 for the restaurant."

"What do you mean, what has happened to the business?"

I did not quite catch what he said as he had a broad Italian accent, but realized only too well what he was trying to tell me. I had left it too late again, and maybe missed my only chance of getting some money back.

Chapter 6

Every effort that I had made had failed.

Thinking seriously about the whole situation I realized that my health was now suffering, and I would have to accept that this man who was a liar, cheat, gambler and a womanizer had finally beaten me.

But I thought well—that's life. My few loyal friends and colleagues continued to tell me all the up-to-date news they would have about him, but now I would just listen and not pursue the facts.

I kept asking myself, had I really come to terms with what had happened?

I had got mad, but I had still not got even. It wrangled me, but as I had passed my 70th birthday, I realized that I had had enough.

We did not talk about Ivica often any more. People would occasionally ask, "Any news of you-know-who recently?" or "Have you gotten your money yet?"

My reply was always the same.

"You must be joking, but maybe one day, you never know, your luck may turn. One thing I'm certain of is that I'll not rest until I do."

Then quite unexpectedly, I received a telephone call from a man who said that he was Ivica's brother-in-law. He told me that he was married to Ivica's sister, and had recently served her with papers for a divorce. I knew of him but had never met nor even spoken to him.

I wondered why he was telephoning me.

"You don't know me, but I hear that you are having a problem locating Ivica."

"Yes that is right but how do you know?"

"Everybody seems to know, and anyway there are so many people besides yourself who want to catch up with him."

"I don't mean to be rude, but you don't know me, so why are you telling me this?"

"Well I have heard how badly Ivica has been treating you, and now his sister, who you know I am still married to—not for much longer I hope—is trying to do the same sort of thing to me."

After talking for a long time on the telephone, I began to realize that this man really wanted to help, albeit in a very small way. He had absolutely nothing to gain from giving me any information, so I thanked him and promised to keep in touch.

What he told me was that Ivica had written an affidavit on behalf of his sister's claim to house, goods, and business. Ivica was to be questioned in court about this in two weeks time, so at least I would know where to find him on that date.

Once again I hoped that something could be done.

I went to see a solicitor for him to arrange for two debt collectors to wait for Ivica outside the court.

As it happened, my husband and I had an appointment in the same town on that day, and by sheer coincidence were passing near the courts on our way back to the car, when my husband said frantically, "Turn around and don't look back. He's just going into the court building."

"I know, I just saw him," I said and quickly started walking the other way.

It was a hard thing to do, but I knew that if I confronted Ivica, I would get so upset, and most likely do or say something that I would later regret. Much better to leave it to the experts—or so I thought.

When I contacted my solicitor to enquire how the two debt collectors had got on, I could not believe my ears. Yes, you've guessed it. They had missed Ivica! Yet another good chance missed.

I later heard from friends that Ivica had been in court all day, and had even spent two hours having lunch in one of his old haunts, where he had been eating and drinking in public with old associates.

I didn't know what to think. Had the two debt collectors been so busy drinking in the pub opposite, that they had forgotten the work in hand, or had I been set up yet again?

It didn't really matter, because I knew that there would not be another opportunity like this for a very long time. What upset me most was that I was again obsessed with the situation, even though a short while before I had decided to try to forget it.

Ivica's brother-in-law kindly let me have a copy of the court transcript. It stated, that during the questioning by the judge, Ivica had confirmed that he was an international businessman, with businesses in three or four countries.

He was asked during the hearing whether he traveled extensively.

"Yes sir I do," he answered.

"And who owns the property where you live in London?"

Most of his answers had been the same as at the oral examination, but during this hearing he was much more hesitant and at times very reticent to answer at all.

As before, he confirmed that he also had another large house on an island in his home country, Yugoslavia.

"So, please tell me, Mr. Kalebic, how are you able to bring large sums of money into this country?"

"Usually in deutschmarks—it is an open currency."

He was then questioned about some of his past businesses in the town.

When asked why his signatures were not the same on all documents, he confirmed that he changed them according to which country he was in.

I have to admit that when I read this I was surprised that the judge had not questioned him further on that point. But he hadn't.

"So how would you describe yourself Mr. Kalebic?"

"As an international entrepreneur, Sir."

The judge coughed, and then put to him that there had been a deliberate decision to remove all his assets from this country. This Ivica denied emphatically.

He again insisted, under oath, that he had neither changed his name nor his religion, and was still a Catholic.

I was pleased to have this information, but doubted that it would help me.

At least Ivica was behaving true to form—lying under oath. But as I have been told repeatedly by the legal authorities, it is not up to Ivica to prove that he is telling the truth. It is up to me to prove that he is lying.

One day maybe I will be able to do this.

Chapter 7

Winter passed as usual, and one evening at the beginning of the following spring, I was sitting reading the local newspaper. Ivica was the furthest thing from my mind.

I had been looking for my horoscope which I read religiously, but when turning over the pages I was struck by the headlines of a full page story.

PROBLEMS IN PARADISE

Echo Investigations earlier this year exposed fraudster businessman. Trail of businessman's debts continue to soar, but he is still living in his luxury home in Florida.

The whole story seemed unbelievable. But what struck my eye was an interesting piece written beside a small photograph of another man, which read, "PRIVATE EYE trails Anderson."

Private detective, Gary Thomas, of Titan Business Services (TBS) has spent months on the trail of the builder and developer. It was only after a lengthy investigation by TBS, which deals in credit and monetary matters, company fraud, and debt recovery, that prompted the police investigation into Anderson's business.

Mr. Thomas said that he planned to persuade Anderson to hand over more than £40,000, when he visited Florida.

He said, "I am going over to the U.S.A. to try to collect £23,000 for one client and £18,000 for another."

This story really impressed me, and I turned to my husband, who was watching TV, and said, "Look at this in the paper. Will you read it and tell me what you think?"

"Can't it wait a minute? I'm watching the news. Anyway what's it about?"

"Well I suppose it can wait but I'd like to know what you think about it now."

I handed my husband the newspaper. He started to read it and then turned and asked me, "What has it got to do with you? Why are you so interested?"

My husband was obviously not the slightest bit interested, because he turned to me and said sternly, "What am I supposed to say, what do you want me to say?"

"It isn't a case of what I want you to say. Do you think that I should contact this private investigator to see if he can try to get my money for me?"

"Oh, we are not on about that again, surely I thought you agreed to forget about it."

"Well I can't, so what do you think I should do?"

"Anyway you are not going to listen to me but, if you want my honest opinion, I think you would be wasting your time, and I suggest that you forget it," he said.

"I've got nothing to lose except the price of a phone call."

"He's not going to be interested in your problem, anyway what do you think that he will be able to do, that all the others haven't?"

"I didn't expect much enthusiasm, but at least give me a little encouragement."

"Lorna, I would really like to, but you know as well as I do what will happen. You will do yourself no good and start up all the worrying and being upset again. Why won't you let sleeping dogs lie? You know it is the best thing to do even if you won't admit it."

"You are probably right, but I still think that I will telephone him tomorrow, if I can get his number."

"Then be it on your own head," my husband said and returned to watching the news on television.

By the morning I had no doubts about trying to contact Mr. Thomas. Eventually, I was able to get his number and when I rang a polite young lady answered.

"TBS Services, can I help you?"

"Could I speak to Mr. Gary Thomas please?"

"Who is speaking?"

"My name is Lorna McBride. He doesn't know me."

"What do you wish to speak to him about?"

"A £60,000 debt which is owing to me."

"If you will hold the line Mrs. McBride, I will see if he is available."

After what seemed an age, but was only a few minutes, a brusque voice on the other end said, "Gary Thomas, here, Mrs. McBride, what can I do to help you?"

Briefly, I explained the whole story to him.

"I quite understand what you are saying to me," he said "but without written proof of what you have told me, I cannot say whether or not I will be able to help you."

"So what do you suggest that I do?"

"Would you be able to come to my office, and bring any documented evidence that you have?"

"That will be no problem."

"Right, then will you make an appointment with Tracy, my secretary, and if you will bring all the relevant files, I will be able to assess the situation much better. Bye, hope to see you soon,"

Later that week my husband and I, armed with boxes of files which had accumulated over the past seven years, arrived at Mr. Thomas' office.

We spent more than an hour with him discussing all things legal and otherwise. When we left, we were tired and not too hopeful, but at least he had been able to give us some encouragement, though very little. He had explained that we were up against some powerful people, but he was prepared to give it a try.

We had parked our car at the side of the police station as it was just across the road from his office.

As we were walking back my husband asked me, "Have you got the car keys?"

"Why should I have them, you were driving?"

"Well I haven't, so what do you suggest that we do now?"

I walked over to the car to see if we had left them inside. Not a sign of them. Anyway we realized that if we had left them in the car, we would not have been able to lock it, and it was securely locked.

As usual we were each blaming the other, when I spotted a note under the front windscreen wiper, which read, "Keys in Police Station."

That seemed strange.

Anyway at the Police Station we were told that our car keys had been found in the hatch back lock, by a young man as he was passing. We had obviously been so concerned about getting all the files out of the back that we had completely forgotten to lock the car. The police had done that for us.

At least it was so nice to realize that there was still an honest youngster about these days. This lad could so easily have vandalized the car, or stolen from it, or even driven it away.

Maybe this was a good omen. Could my luck be changing at last? I would just have to wait and see.

The next day Gary Thomas telephoned me to say that having looked through all the evidence we had given him, he was prepared to work on my behalf, and do all that he could to try to get some, if not all of the money owed to me.

I was delighted and said so.

"Yes, but you have to remember Mrs. McBride, it is going to be a long and very hard job and, in the end, all the hard work could prove totally fruitless."

"I quite understand that, but as I told you when I came to see you, I have no money to pay you."

"I know that, but as I explained to you at our meeting, we can make arrangements about payment later. Usually we say, no results, no charge, so until we can get some money for you, we do not expect to be paid."

This sounded encouraging, although most unusual to me. But then I had not had dealings with this sort of person before.

"What will your fees be if you are successful?"

"Twenty percent of any of the monies retrieved, and we usually deduct this before we make any payment to you."

"That sounds fair enough to me. Now do you want me to sign a contract with you?"

"Not at this stage. All I need is a verbal agreement, so that I can get on with the job straight away."

"As far as I'm concerned you can do all that you think is necessary. When you need any further information, just ring, and if I'm not available, leave a message on the answering machine, and I'll get back to you as soon as I can. If I can help you in any way let me know—remember I have been collecting facts for the past eight years, so I have lots of other information that might help, and save you a lot of time."

"I'll remember that. My assistants and I will get on with this investigation straight away I promise you. Expect to hear from me in about a week to let you know how we are getting on."

"You don't know how much I appreciate what you are doing for me. Will speak to you soon. Bye."

I had now learned to trust no-one, but somehow I felt that this man had to be the exception. Was I right? This had been my decision alone, and although everything still seemed stacked against me, I somehow knew that he would work hard on my behalf.

Chapter 8

Two days later I received a copy of a letter which had been sent by TBS to Ivica. It read:

Dear Mr. Kalebic,

We write to you in connection with your outstanding High Court Judgment obtained by our client, Mrs. McBride of Cardiff. I must inform you that we are now in the process of issuing a Bankruptcy Order against you. The amount owed is £59,897.

This includes further interest and costs. We are also starting criminal proceedings against you for obtaining money by deception, and we will also be reporting you to the C.S.A. and the D.H.S.S., because we believe that you have committed offences against those acts too.

I think it only fair to inform you that there is going to be a large amount of publicity in the national press, who feel that it will make a good story as one of your daughters is already in the public eye, and because of the well known family that you have married into.

You left Wales without a thought to the damage that you had done to our client, and have made no attempt to put right any of the financial difficulties you put her in, not to mention the mental anguish.

Obviously you thought that this matter had blown over and gone away, but I can assure you that we are not going to let it drop. We feel that you are in a strong financial position and should make good your promise to pay the money you owe to our client, and if you have any sense of decency you will do so right away. This letter is not an idle threat, and we aim to bring this matter to the highest authority.

Should you or your legal representatives need to contact me, you can do so on any of the above numbers.

Yours sincerely,

TBS

Waiting for any reply seemed endless. Gary (we were now on first term names having spoken so often) telephoned me every day to keep me informed of what was going on.

"Lorna, Gary Thomas, here, I've arranged for some journalists from the national press to call to interview you on Thursday of this week. Is that OK with you?"

"Well yes…, but I have no idea what they will expect me to say."

"Don't worry. Just tell them the story exactly as you have told it to me. Shall I tell them to call about 11:00 o'clock?"

"Yes, that will be fine. I'll leave everything to you."

"Right, I'll be in touch. Bye."

When I came off the telephone I found it difficult to come to terms with the developments, but knew that if I gave up now I'd lose any chance I might have of getting any of my money.

The representatives from the papers duly arrived as arranged on the following Thursday—one journalist and a photographer.

I invited them into the sitting room, offered them a cup of coffee and waited.

Having never been in a situation like this before, I felt it better if I were to let them ask me questions. Then I could answer.

"That is not the way we like to do things, Mrs. McBride, just tell us your story and we will take it from there."

"Right, well," and taking a deep breath told the story as I had so many times before, but usually on deaf ears.

After we had been talking for about an hour, the journalist turned to the photographer, who had been sitting in complete silence during the interview and said, "Will you go with Mr. McBride and get some photographs of the cottage that was lost through the debt."

"Yes, that is a good idea; it should save us some time. How far is it from here?"

Turning to me the journalist asked, "Will it take them long to get there?"

"It's about 14 miles, and should take about twenty five minutes, that's if there are no holdups. These days you never know."

So the photographer and my husband set off for the village where the cottage was.

Whilst they were gone the journalist and I continued to discuss the whole story. He showed great interest, especially when he realized that Ivica's daughter was a regular Page Three girl.

The photographer and my husband were away for almost an hour and a half and when they returned they wanted photographs taken of me standing by our garden gate.

This took far longer than I had expected. I had thought that the photographer would take one or two photographs, but he needed at least twenty. I cannot understand to this day why, because not one was used, although I am sure that they did not know that at the time.

It was at least another two hours before they left, assuring me that one of the national newspapers would run the story within a week or so.

He left me his business card and various telephone numbers so that I could contact him at any time should I have any queries, or new relevant information.

When they had gone, although I felt more optimistic about things, I still wondered whether I was doing the right thing.

Would there be repercussions on my family and friends? I thought a lot about this, but realized that it was too late now to turn back.

It was now several hours since they had left. I tried hard to put the whole affair out of my mind, at least for a couple of days. I could not discuss it too much as everybody was insisting that what I had done was entirely my own choice.

I knew this only too well but it did not make the situation any easier for me.

Everybody seemed so convinced that I was wasting my time. I have to admit that at times, so was I.

Chapter 9

The following morning, Gary telephoned me. Hearing his voice always made me feel better.

"Well, Lorna how did things go, did they turn up?"

"Yes they did, and what's more they seemed very interested."

"Good. Now I have some more news for you. I've just been on to our national paper," he was of course referring to the Welsh one.

Gary continued, "Would you be prepared to talk to their journalist? I know it is asking a lot of you, but if you remember I told you in the beginning that it was not going to be easy, and the only way that I can see you getting any of your money is by putting all the pressure we can on them at the some time.

"They have far more influence in all quarters than we have, but this at least might make them sit up and take notice. Let's hope so anyway. So can I arrange for Sion, that's the journalist, to call at your house on Sunday?"

"Yes, will two o'clock suit him? I have to go out in the morning."

Gary hesitated and then said, "Sion is here with me now and he says that will be fine."

"Will it be the same sort of interview that I had last Thursday with the other fellow?"

"Yes, but this should be much easier for you. I know this man very well, and most people find him very pleasant to deal with. I'll keep you informed of any developments. Bye, and thanks a lot."

As I might have expected, things became hectic, at least seemed they to be for an old age pensioner like myself living in the country.

During the next few days, I was contacted by the BBC and asked if I would appear on a television show—a woman's magazine wanted to buy the story for a negotiable fee—and several freelance writers put offers to me.

But to each I had to give the same answer, "I'm sorry, but, at the moment, I have a private investigator acting on my behalf, so I am afraid that you will have to contact him."

"We already have, and he told us that we have to speak to you."

"Then maybe you would like to ring me at a later date, when l have had time to think things over and have decided what I am going to do. But thank you for your interest, and for contacting me."

The television people, although very polite, were more concerned to know there and then whether I would or would not do the show. I was not prepared to give an answer without giving it some serious thought.

It would have meant that I would have to travel to London, and, as it was a long journey, I was not prepared to do.

I was offered chauffeured transport to the studio, but I was worried, and felt that I would not be able to cope with a live interview after having traveled so far. Gary had gone to such a lot of trouble to organize this and I felt so sorry that I had to let him down.

"I quite understand Lorna, don't worry about it. The pity is that it would have given your story so much publicity."

"I know, but I wouldn't want to look an utter fool. Maybe they could record it at the local television centre in Cardiff. That is only about ten miles from my home. It would only take me about half an hour to get there and I would feel far more comfortable."

"I'll try and arrange it for you but I doubt very much that they will agree, as they like to have this type of program going out live."

Many days of discussion followed, and a very agreeable lady from the London centre said, that if I would be prepared to travel to Manchester, then maybe they could arrange something there where I would feel far more comfortable.

"Thank you for all your consideration, I really appreciate it, but I would like a little time to think about it, and promise that I will let you know very soon."

Finally I agreed to do the interview in Manchester providing they could not find an alternative, and suggested that they make all further arrangements through Gary.

Thursday arrived and so did Sion. He had asked me a few days before whether my daughter could be present at the interview, so that she could confirm some of the facts that I would be giving him. Trudy agreed.

He arrived alone as the photographer who was to have come with him had been taken on an urgent story. It was arranged that the photographs could be taken on another day, and eventually they were—this time only outside the cottage.

To get back to the interview, Sion asked all the same sort of questions as I had been asked before. These I was beginning to know by heart, as I had answered them so many times.

When the interview finished, Sion said to both of us, "Thank you for your help. I think that I have all the information that I need, and hopefully, Mrs. McBride, if I can get the approval of my editor, your story should be in print within a week."

"That would be marvelous, but I have had so many promises, that I can't really believe that it will happen."

"I can assure you that unless something goes radically wrong it will. I'll let you know what day it will be in the paper."

When he left, I dare not think that this time it might finally be in print.

I was elated, and although I was very tired, felt that I had to ring Gary with the latest news. After all, without his help, I would not even have got this far.

"Gary, I can't really believe that they will be interested enough to print the story."

"Knowing Sion, if that is what he told you, then I am sure he will keep his word if he can. Anyway, I have a lot of other things in motion. As I told you the other day, I am sending letters and copies of them, to all the relevant commissions etc. So far I have not had any replies, but I will expect some reaction after the story hits the papers."

Sion proved to be a man of his word and, on the following Thursday, the story was printed in the National Paper of Wales. I was surprised to see the prominence that it had been given. I had expected a small paragraph just outlining the details. But no! It had a full half broadsheet devoted to it, complete with three large photographs. One of myself alongside Ivica who was wearing a type of fez and his wife a jeweled headdress.

Anyone who saw it must have wondered what the connection was between this elderly pensioner, and the other two young affluent looking people.

They would soon know once they had read the story. At long last the truth was in print. This was another date that I might want to remember, or maybe forget. We would have to wait and see.

I had rushed to buy several copies of the paper at our local airport— which incidentally is our nearest newsagent. The people in the shop who saw me most mornings, when I called for the papers having walked our dog, seemed surprised at the number of copies that I bought, but did not pass comment, and as I had not yet read the contents, neither did I.

The newspaper was dated. Thursday, 23rd March. 1995, and the story ran as follows.

DEBT CASE: Welsh pensioner owed £59,000 by relative of the world's richest man.

SULTAN'S RELATION REFUSES TO REPAY LOAN

The husband of the niece of the world's richest man, the Sultan of Brunei, owes a Welsh pensioner more than £59,000 and despite having a High Court Judgment for repayment of the debt against

Ivica Kalebic now known as Adam Bin Ibrahim, Mrs. Lorna McBride has yet to receive a penny.

The debt involves a £25,000 bank loan for which Mrs. McBride of Cardiff acted as guarantor for Mr. Kalebic's part in a hotel venture.

At the time, Mrs. McBride's daughter, Trudy, was in a relationship with Mr. Kalebic, and they had a son, Alexander, now aged ten. As collateral for Mr. Kalebic's loan, Mrs. McBride put up her grandmother's cottage in Taffswell, near Cardiff, and which was intended to be sold as a pension nest egg for herself and husband Eric. However within three weeks of Mrs. McBride's signing over the deeds of the cottage, The Kings Hotel in Newport was put into voluntary liquidation in October 1986.

After assurances from Croatian-born Mr. Kalebic 47 that the loan would be repaid, Mrs. McBride agreed to extend her guarantee on the initial three month loan until she reached retirement age. However, the day before Mrs. McBride arranged for herself and Mr. Kalebic to go to the bank to redeem the deeds on her grandmother's cottage he disappeared.

Mrs. McBride then discovered from the bank that none of the £25,000 loan had been repaid, and in fact it amounted to £30,000. Liable for the outstanding repayment, Mrs. McBride was forced to sell her cottage in Taffswell quickly at much less than its market price.

Despite exhaustive efforts to trace Mr. Kalebic, known as Yogiit, or John Kalebic in South Wales' casino and business circles, it was more than a year before the two finally met up at Cardiff's Celtic Bay Hotel.

Here in October 1989 Mr. Kalebic, who moved from the former Yugoslavia in the late 1960's, signed a statement acknowledging his debt of £30,000 to Mrs. McBride.

In a twist to the story, in August 1990, Mr. Kalebic married the niece of the Sultan of Brunei, Siti Mariam Isa.

The couple first met when the Sultan's niece was studying architecture in Cardiff. Their lavish marriage in the oil rich state of Brunei lasted four days and was attended by guests from all over the world.

As one of many expensive wedding gifts, Mr. Kalebic received a Rolex watch worth £10,000.

Incensed by his new found status Mrs. McBride finally secured a High Court Judgment against Mr. Kalebic for £38,057.57p.

In May 1991, with a daily interest rate of £11.78, the debt today stands at £59,896.86p.

However Mr. Kalebic, despite marrying into the richest family in the world, claimed under oath that he is penniless and therefore unable to pay his debt.

While in Britain, Mr. Kalebic and his second wife lived in an exclusive house at Porchester Terrace, London, and employed a maid.

Payments for the running of the Porchester Terrace house are made by a company called Merindah Ltd.

However, a letter to Mrs. McBride from solicitors Jaques and Lewis, acting on behalf of Merindah Ltd and the Sultan's advisor Mr. Ibrahim, stated that neither 55 Porchester Terrace nor its contents belonged to Mr. Kalebic.

A BMW car with his personalized number plate YOGIIT, Mr. Kalebic claimed was given to his wife. He added that his wife gave him money when he needed it.

Mrs. McBride, who has spent £8,000 on legal fees in her fight against Mr. Kalebic, has now turned to Newport based private detective and Falklands veteran Gary Thomas of Titan Business Services in a final effort to get justice.

Having read so far as you can well imagine, I was so pleased that my problem was now public, but a little apprehensive not knowing what the outcome might be.

Over the previous months, I had been hearing from various sources that Ivica had been telling his friends not to listen to that "batty old dear" any more as he had paid her the money.

This, I repudiated by paying the same newspaper to print in their legal section that I had not. The only reaction that I had from it was to know that some of his friends were beginning to have doubts about his credibility, so they said. To return to the article in the paper, it read:

GRANDMOTHER LEFT BROKEN HEARTED
AND ALMOST DESTITUTE

Having worked in a family antiques business, Lorna McBride was looking forward to a well-earned secure retirement with husband Eric.

But one man was to shatter those hopes and leave her almost destitute.

The man is Ivica Kalebic now married to the Sultan of Brunei's niece, and at one time was Mrs. McBride's daughter's lover.

It was back in 1982 that Trudy McBride, now happily married, first met Mr. Kalebic.

At the time he was still married to his first wife Pat Kalebic of Rhiwbina. From that marriage Mr. Kalebic had two children. However, love soon blossomed between Mr. Kalebic and the solicitor Miss Trudy McBride. They set up home together, and had a son Alexander. Ivica was plausible, but we were suspicious as he was known as a gambler and a womanizer, reflected Mrs. McBride.

Unknown to Trudy McBride, Mr. Kalebic approached her mother asking her to stand guarantor to a short term £25,000 bank loan. "1 did not read the document and just signed not realizing that it was a mortgage agreement.

"In hindsight I should have got legal advice, but Ivica stressed that it would only be a short term arrangement," said Mrs. McBride. More than a decade later, Mrs. McBride has not received a penny back. With interest Ivica is now indebted to his song grandmother to the tune of £59,000.

Mrs. McBride revealed, "The whole affair has broken my heart. Sometimes I think of giving it up. However my anger and hurt quickly return and I realize that I have to fight on-even if it kills me."

With tears in her eyes, Mrs. McBride continued, "If Ivica was an ordinary man I might have thought, well that is just my hard luck.

"However when I think of the wealth that he has married into, I find it disgusting and insulting that he claims that he has not got money to pay me."

With Mrs. McBride having to pay off Mr. Kalebic's £30,000 outstanding debt, she has suffered both financially and physically.

"The cottage in Taffswell was going to be used as mine and my husband's retirement nest, as we did not have any pensions. Losing my house to cover the loan has meant that everyday life for us has been a struggle. I have spent all my savings on legal fees. If it was not for the help of my family, we would be destitute. Ivica has ruined my life," said Mrs. McBride.

The pensioner has lost over two stone in weight and admits that her health has been adversely affected.

Despite protests, Mrs. McBride said her grievance had fallen on deaf ears at the Brunei High Commission and the Home Office. "If I had the money I would travel to Brunei to tell the Sultan himself what the husband of his niece has done to me. The Sultan is renowned for his charity and integrity and I believe he would not knowingly allow someone like Ivica to disgrace his name in such a way."

Among Mr. Kalebic's businesses which he no longer owns were The Debrovonic, and Frenchman restaurants, the Night Club Bananas, and The Millers Mate pub.

Chapter 10

In 1995, for the next few days, friends, relations etc., were telephoning to give me any support that they could. Believe me, I needed it and it helped to know that some people at least were thinking of me.

The following Sunday morning during breakfast the telephone rang. Should I answer it or not?

My husband suggested that whoever it was could leave a message on the answering machine if it was urgent.

"Oh, I don't know. I'd better answer it," I said, "in case it is one of the family and they may wonder why we are not at home at this time on a Sunday morning."

"Alright, that's up to you, but whoever it is don't give any information."

Imagine my shock when I heard Ivica's voice at the other end of the line.

He was the last person that I had expected to hear from. "Hello Lorna, this is Ivica, how are you?"

"You know how. I am not at all well."

"Why, what is the matter?"

"You have the nerve to ask me that after all you are putting me through."

"You know I have no money to pay you."

"Shall I tell you something Ivica? I don't believe anything that you say any more."

"I know about all that is in the paper, and want to know why you are doing this to me?" said Ivica.

"I'll tell you why. Because you have crucified me during the past seven years. You have lied and cheated—and you have the audacity to ask me why!"

Up until then he had seemed quite calm, but suddenly he became threatening and abusive.

Now Ivica was literally screaming on the telephone.

"Do you realize that you have ruined my life, broken up my marriage, made me lose everything including my new lifestyle?"

And, as if he could not control himself and wanted to say anything that could hurt me, he blurted out, "Alexander is no longer my son; I don't know him any more. How do I know that he ever was?"

This hurt me more than anything. To think that a man would use his own son as a means to get what he wanted.

By this time he was not prepared to listen to anything that I said. I suggested that we could all meet and talk about the debt. He continued to shout. At the same time my husband was telling me to put the phone down, but I felt that at least I had some sort of contact with him at the moment which was more than I usually had.

He then became almost obscene and completely irrational, and his voice became uncontrollable, "If you don't stop doing this to me I'll send a video of Trudy and me to all her legal colleagues. I'll ruin her. Have you forgotten that you refused an offer of £20,000 that I made you nearly three years ago?"

"That is where you are wrong Ivica. That solicitor who was working for someone, and I was never told for whom, categorically withdrew that offer. He said that he was not able to negotiate for his client."

Ivica had now become so incoherent that it was totally impossible to carry on any sort of conversation with him. I was getting so upset that I had to put the telephone down. I went back to the breakfast table shaken, but it was along time before I felt able to repeat the whole saga to my husband.

"What on earth is he talking about?" asked my husband. "Have you ever heard of any videos or suchlike, when they were living in Farm Drive?"

"Never, but—at the moment I can't really think straight. When I feel a bit calmer, I'll ring Trudy and tell her what he said. Maybe she'll be able to shed some light on it, and know what he is on about. Just because we have not heard about it, doesn't mean to say that he has not got anything...although I doubt it.

"What do you suggest I do?"

"Nothing until you have spoken to Trudy"

I worried all morning and decided to resolve the whole thing as quickly as possible.

I telephoned Trudy at lunchtime hoping that she would be at home.

"Hello....oh, it's you Mum any news?"

I told her about the telephone conversation that I had with Ivica earlier in the morning.

"What are you going to do about it, Mum?"

"Firstly, tell me the truth, are there any videos that Ivica has and could use to blackmail us?"

"Not that I'm aware of. If you want my advice, personal not legal, I would say call his bluff. As far as I am concerned he hasn't anything that he could use."

"Then, if you are sure, I'll take your advice and do that, but you know that I would not want to do anything that would jeopardize your career."

"Don't worry Mum, just sit and wait, he'll not do anything."

"I wish that I could be so sure, Trudy."

Waiting was not easy, but I felt that I had asked for my daughter's advice so I should take it.

The next day I told Gary what had happened. He said, "Now Ivica is threatening and trying his best to intimidate you. Try and put it out of your mind for a while and I will deal with it."

When the post arrived the next morning, there was a copy of a letter that Gary had sent to Ivica, and it read:

I write to you again in connection with your outstanding High Court writ for money you owe to our client Mrs. McBride. You have not seen fit to contact me at my office about this matter as I requested, but you did make an abusive phone call to our client at her home.

I must inform you that the conversation was taped, and we are looking at it with a view to handing it over to the proper authorities. If you wish to discuss this matter with anyone, please do so, only through this office and myself.

As I have already pointed out, we are in the process of having the matter of how you used the money obtained from our client, looked at with the view of bringing a possible charge of obtaining money by deception, we are also in the process of issuing bankruptcy proceedings against you personally.

We have enclosed copies of an article in one of our National newspapers here in Wales and we will be going on National television on one of the consumer programs shortly, as they feel that it is a good story and will be of public interest.

We have also been contacted by some of the National tabloids asking if we would be prepared to talk to them and the family that you have married into.

I am quite sure that you do not wish yours or you present family's name to be dragged through the press, but our client insists she gets justice, and if this drastic course of action is the only way left to her, then she is prepared to do so.

You can however stop this action immediately by fulfilling your obligations to our client. If you do so all proceedings against you will be dropped.

Please contact me on any of the above numbers if you wish to discuss any of these points.

Gary was certainly keeping up the pressure by repeating the facts to him, as often as possible, and told me when I spoke to him later in the day that at the same time as he had sent the letter to Ivica, he had sent this one. It read:

For the attention of His Royal Highness. The Sultan of Brunei. The Brunei High Commission.

17-19 Belgrave Square, London.

Please find copies of documents sent to Ivica. Kalebic - Adam Bin Ibrahim, to which as yet we have had no reply.

We hope that by bringing this matter to your attention, you may be able to use any influence you may have, to get Mr. Kalebic to resolve this matter.

We also feel it only fair to inform you of the adverse publicity being attached to this case, caused by Mr. Kalebic's refusal to do the honorable thing and put right the pain and heartache he caused when he left Wales and our client behind. Some of the articles written are enclosed.

Any help that you can give to our client would be very much appreciated. You can also contact me on any of the above numbers should you wish, if you require any further information.

For the next week things seemed to get chaotic. This system did not seem to be bringing any results. There were telephone calls all through the days and into the evenings, but nothing satisfactory developed.

Then, when I was least expecting it, Gary telephoned and said, "Lorna, you'll be pleased to know that we have at last made contact. We must have rattled somebody's cage, because a solicitor called John Watton rang me and said that they would be prepared to negotiate a deal."

"What sort of deal?"

"Well apparently they have a client, who they say is a very influential businessman in the city, who is prepared to buy the Judgment for £20,000.

"Did they give you the name of this man?"

"No they didn't. In fact they refused point blank, why I don't know, but they seem eager to come to a settlement as soon as possible."

"This must be the same solicitor who tried to negotiate an agreement a year or two ago. I wouldn't trust him further than I can see him, and anyway why is he being so cagey?"

"Shall we see what he has to offer? We can't lose anything by it."

"I will leave it entirely up to you, go ahead and we will wait and see what happens."

Gary contacted this man by fax, and he said that he would forward a copy of an initial agreement to him and one to the solicitor who was acting for Gary and for me.

Later that day I called to see the solicitor, a lady, at her office, so that I could read the agreement, and decide what we would do about it. It was totally unacceptable to me, so I suggested that if they were prepared to make sensible alterations I might consider accepting their offer, otherwise I was not interested.

Chapter 11

It seemed so strange to me. I was the injured party, had lost £59,000, and yet they were making all the conditions. I realized by now that it might be better to accept something, which would be better than I had so far, which was absolutely nothing.

Then they listed all the conditions to which I was bound to adhere.

All publicity had to stop immediately.

Newspaper articles, television interviews also.

I was not even to discuss what was going on with anybody outside the people directly concerned.

Providing that they added no more ridiculous conditions, I told Gary that I would probably be prepared to come to some arrangement with them.

Once Gary had told John Watton this, Watton made it known to Gary that they were not prepared to pay the full amount owing to me under ANY conditions.

So now I really had to think long and hard and make up my mind what I was going to do.

I was now over 70 years old. I was getting very tired and fed up with the whole situation. Each day it seemed to get worse. Should I count my losses and accept a much lesser amount? If I didn't, I was sure that they would fight me all the way, and they had ample money and influence to do this.

Some of my family and friends were now saying, stick it out.

You have got this far, maybe they will change their minds and pay you the full amount,

I eventually decided that I could not risk it, and asked Gary to try to get the best that he could for me.

He now had my complete trust.

Not many hours later he received this fax from John Watton. It read:

Re. Ivica Kalebic:

I refer to our fresh discussions and have pleasure in enclosing herewith draft deed and draft notice.

It is essential that Mrs. McBride and her daughter obtain independent legal advice, and I note that you will insure that this is done.

I understand that your practice has been in touch with the Brunei High Commission making certain allegations. Could you let me have a copy of such correspondence, and on completion of the proposed transaction, my client would like a letter from your practice addressed to the Brunei High Commission confirming this matter has been amicably settled and acknowledging that you and your clients recognize that Ivica's wife Siti. Mariam Isa. is not a member of the Sultan of Brunei's family.

Can you please let me have a draft of such letter together with draft copies of previous correspondence?

When replying, could you please let me have your undertaking that you and your practice will keep this agreement confidential, and that you will not directly or indirectly contact or attempt to contact Mr. Kalebic or his business associate or partners and/or Mr.

Kalebic's family and that you will not give any further publicity direct or indirectly to all or any of the transactions, dealings or events between Mrs. McBride, her daughter and/or Mr. Kalebic Finally my client also requires an undertaking from your practice not to act for any other party pursuing claims against Mr. Kalebic.

I look forward to hearing from you and /or your solicitors.

When I read this I was appalled by the audacity of this man. I telephoned Gary as soon as I got home.

70

"How on earth can they put these ludicrous restrictions forward? It's bad enough that they are trying to GAG me, but to try to tell you what you can and cannot do in my own business is completely inexcusable. It's appalling."

"I agree with you Lorna, and believe me I'm as mad as hell, but for your sake, I am trying my best to get him to compromise. As we have said all along it is you who is the injured party, and they are dictating all the rules."

"That is the whole problem. I dare not think what their reaction would be if the tables were turned," I said.

"I'll have to get in touch with Karen (the solicitor acting for us), and try to clarify the legality of it all."

"Thanks Gary, but I'd like you to know that I don't expect you to agree to anything that will jeopardize your future business."

"Don't worry about that. I know you wouldn't. Leave it with me and I'll be in touch," replied Gary.

Telephone and fax messages were numerous during the next few days. We could not really understand what was happening because now the people acting for Ivica, albeit indirectly, seemed to want to settle this matter as quickly as possible.

What had changed? For many months they had completely ignored all letters etc. Now, time seemed to be very important to them, but they still insisted on making the rules.

Was somebody in much higher authority instructing them? Maybe they had too much to lose if they did not get the problem sorted out.

We tried all ways to find out but, as always, had no success.

Within a day or two I received this fax which had been sent from Karen through my daughter's office:

I enclose a draft letter to John Watton. Please let me have your comments. I have not yet amended the agreement, but I think we might as well get their comments on this matter first.

If you want to speak to me over the weekend I will be working on Sunday and can be contacted on my business telephone number.

The draft enclosure read as follows.

We act on behalf of Triton Business Services in connection with the terms of the draft agreement you have forwarded to him. We are in receipt of the draft agreement, Consent notice of application and your letter of the 11th May, 1995.

We make the following points:-

1. We understand that you refused to state who your client is. We do not think that it is acceptable to proceed on this basis, and we require you to confirm to us who you are acting for. We note that a company called Centron is to enter into the agreement. We are also aware that Mr. John Watton is a director of this company.

We take a view that such an interest of your firm in this matter should have been disclosed.

2. We do not understand why you want the plaintiff's daughter to be joined in as a party to this agreement.

She is not a party to the court proceedings, and has no interest in them.

In any event Trudy McBride is clearly unable to agree to the contents of paragraphs 4 and 6 of the draft agreement since she and Mr. Kalebic have a child together.

3. As regards the payment of the sum of £20,000 there appears to be an error in paragraph 2. of the draft agreement which refers to date in paragraph 6.

We are of the view that the sum of £20,000 should be paid upon Mrs. McBride's signing of the agreement.

We suggest that the simplest solution is for you to send us your client cheque for £20,000, made payable to ourselves, which we will clear through our account, and hold to your order until we have posted to you the agreement executed by Mrs. McBride. Further we do not like the wording of clause 8, since we are doubtful that the court will have the protection of clause 9 if there is anything further which needs to be executed.

We therefore think that clause 8. can be amended so that Mrs. L. McBride will consent to your notice in the form annexed to the agreement.

In respect of the £5,000 paid by the 30th September, 1995, it is not acceptable for Mrs. L. McBride to rely upon Centron paying the sum due.

We are informed that the agreement that you discussed with Mr. Thomas, and that you have previously put forward, is that you will underwrite the payment.

Therefore in respect of this second sum, we will need your undertaking that you hold the sum of £5000 in your client account to our order, and that you will forward your client cheque to us by the 30th September, 1995, made payable to us or to Mrs. McBride.

I will not write a copy of the original draft deed, but having read through these letters carefully my first thought was "what a lot of legal jargon," but was later assured that it was not. Apparently, I was told that one word in the wrong place in the legal profession can drastically alter the concept of an agreement, or even a situation.

I had to accept the reasoning put forward, but felt that if they added any more restrictions, I would have to reconsider my acceptance.

I was kept informed of all the arguments and discussions that were going on, but felt it better not to interfere, and to let the experts deal with them.

Chapter 12

I couldn't rest. Each day I would wait for the post. If nothing arrived, I would wonder why. If there was any news, it did not seem to be the sort that I wanted to hear.

The same with the telephone calls. In the end the only peace I could seem to get, was when I was away from the house.

Now it seemed as if history was repeating itself. We had got so far and no further.

I was now finding it difficult to believe that something was really being achieved.

I was remembering one occasion when I had felt confident that an agreement could be reached.

It was three years before. Maybe at that time I was a little complacent.

All had seemed to be going well, when out of the blue, I received a letter from the second secretary on behalf of the Brunei High Commisioner. It stated:

I received your faxed communications regarding, Mr. Ivica Kalebic, who is now Adam Bin Ibrahim. For your information, this matter is now being handled by the lawyer of Mr. Kalebic and the High Commission does not wish to be involved.

Despite Ivica's persistent denials that he had not changed his name, or had at least acquired another one, even under oath, this had now been admitted by the Brunei High Commission.

I was expecting something like this to happen again, so how was I to believe that what this last solicitor was offering was any more genuine.

He had withdrawn his offer three years before without any warning.

Will he do the same again, I thought, and I'll end up without a penny—after all that had been Ivica's prediction. In my better moments, I was determined to prove him wrong. My intention had always been, not to get angry, just to get even.

This was, so far, proving impossible.

Again there was nothing I could do except wait.

Although it was only a few days later before I heard from Karen, the time seemed endless.

She rang and said, "Lorna, its Karen here. I'm sure you have been expecting me to get in touch, but it wasn't until today that I received a fax from London, I promise I'll put it in the post today—first class, so you should get it in the morning. When you have read it, will you ring me and tell me what you think?"

"I'll do that and thanks a lot for ringing. Bye."

The letter arrived by the morning post as we had hoped. I could not believe that they could find so much to write about all the time.

Were they using more delaying tactics or was this normal negotiating? No wonder legal work costs so much.

I had to read it so made myself a cup of coffee, sat down and read the document:

This is IVICA KALEBIC. WITHOUT PREJUDICE.

We thank you for your letter of the 15th May, We note you are instructed by Triton Business Service. Can you also confirm that you are instructed by Mrs. Lorna McBride and by Trudy McBride.

1. It has also been made perfectly clear that we are instructed by Centron Management Ltd. This company is owned by Mr. John Watton of the practice. Centron Management is acting as nominee for a business associate of Mr. Kalebic.

We do not act for Mr. Kalebic.

2. There is no benefit in reaching a settlement with Mrs. McBride if the daughter were to claim any sums against Mr. Kalebic.

Therefore Trudy McBride needs to confirm that she has no claim whatsoever against Mr. Kalebic, but such waiver is not to extend to any claims in respect of the child that Trudy McBride and Ivica Kalebic might have had.

(I have to say at this point that the last remark was most offensive and unnecessary. Not only was the father's name on the birth certificate, but Ivica's paternity has never been in question.)

Anyway back to the fax. It continued:

Will you please revise/prepare the relevant document and obtain from Trudy McBride, that she approves the same and is willing to enter into the same, and that she has been independently advised.

Such agreement with Trudy McBride is, to provide that she will not contact Ivica Kalebic or make any attempt to contact him save in connection with the said child.

3&4.We are in funds for payment of £25,000, but you will appreciate that these funds do not belong to Mr. Kalebic.

The sum of £20,000 will be paid once the court has made the appropriate order substituting Centron for Lorna McBride as plaintiff in the proceedings -see clause 8. of the draft deed.

We would be agreeable to letting you have simultaneously with completion of the deeds, two cheques drawn on our client account for £20,000 and £5,000 made payable to your firm with the first cheque dated simultaneously with the deed, and the second dated 30th September 1995, and for you to hold such sums as stakeholder according with the terms of the deed. Therefore as soon as the Court Order is made, the £20,000 would be paid by you to your Clients.

On the 30th September 1995, you would be in a position to release £5000 immediately unless at that time you receive notice that your clients have been in breach, and therefore there would be no liability to make any further payments to them. In which case the funds would have to be returned to us, or for you to hold it pending the outcome of any litigation.

In our letter of the 11th May to Mr. Thomas, we made it clear that Mrs. McBride and her daughter must obtain independent legal advice and we await confirmation on this point.

In our letter of the 11th May we requested a letter from Triton to the Brunei High Commission. Mr. Thomas confirmed this was agreeable, although he wanted to state "blood relative" rather than "a member of the Sultan's family. The retraction has to match what was originally published.

I note your client is sending a draft of the proposed letter for consideration, together with copies of the letters sent.

Mr. Thomas confirmed the contents of the fifth paragraph, of our letter regarding confidentiality etc. Again please let us have a draft undertaking which Mr. Thomas/Triton will write.

Mr. Thomas declined to give the undertaking that Triton would not act for any other party with claims against Mr. Kalebic, but said that he would not actively pursue the same. This is unacceptable to our clients in the overall context of this transaction. Mr. Thomas/Triton giving up pursuing Mr. Kalebic on behalf of other creditors is a small price to pay. There are lots of other creditors in the world.

Mr. Thomas of Triton has telephoned us again, and we have spoken to him. Please confirm you consent to our speaking to your client. We look forward to hearing from you.

This was signed as always by the same man. Each time I read it I wondered why everything had to be kept so secret. What were they all afraid of?

Who was this businessman who was prepared to pay off part of the debt? What had he to gain, and why did he not want to be identified?

Was he straightforward and honest, or did he have something to hide? Surely, there had to be a serious reason, but by now it wreaked of subterfuge. As always the ball still seemed to be in their court. It was becoming quite ridiculous. The solicitor, John Watton, and whoever was instructing him, were still being so unreasonable about the conditions.

Chapter 13

I was still owed £60,000. They were offering me just about a third, out of which I would have to pay all fees etc. to the people who were working on my behalf.

I decided to write to the men myself, in plain English that anybody should be able to understand:

Dear Mr. Watton:

With reference to my claim against Mr. Kalebic, I have instructed Mr. Gary Thomas of Triton Business Services to act on my behalf.

Mr. Thomas has my full authority to make any agreement he feels is in my interest.

Also acting on my behalf is Miss Karen Ellis (solicitor) who also acts for Triton Business Services and I am quite happy to go along with any recommendations they might make on my behalf.

As for the conditions you have set against Mr. Thomas, and Triton Business Services, he feels that these are unacceptable to his company. On condition that I get my money, I am prepared for Mr. Thomas to take whatever action he feels necessary to recover it.

I feel it only fair to point out to you very clearly, that the conditions you propose are not relevant to my settlement, and I am prepared to wait until Mr. Thomas is fully satisfied.

As always the following waiting days seemed like a lifetime. Discussions were had between all concerned except of course, the person responsible for it all. Ivica as always was unavailable and "out of the country." When I made any enquiries about him, no one was prepared to give me any information.

Rumors were rife, as always at a time like this.

A friend telephoned in great agitation one morning and said, "Have you heard the latest? A friend rang me earlier and said that she had heard that they have got rid of him."

"Who is supposed to have got rid of him?"

It was quite obvious who she was referring to.

"I'll give you three guesses, but I'm sure you will get it in one."

"They wouldn't dare!" I said.

"You must be joking, who would ever know. You of all people should have learned over the past few years how things can be kept secret and hidden; if you have sufficient money and influence."

I couldn't deny that and remembered a letter I had received through my MP from the Home Office, which read, "Records relating to foreign nationals are confidential, and it is contrary to our practice to disclose information from them to a third party."

They did add that although they had no knowledge of his present address, they had no reason to suppose that he was in this country illegally.

They also wrote that, "The Home Office has had no contact with Mr. Kalebic since 1970."

This seemed a most unusual admission. If they had nothing to hide, why were they so reticent about answering my one simple enquiry?

"What is his nationality now that he is divorced from his first wife?"

He had been allowed to stay and work in this country as long as he was married to a British subject—at least that is what I had been given to understand.

Had the situation changed now that Ivica was divorced?

The people in authority told me quite categorically that I was not entitled to know.

So that was that.

When next I spoke to Gary, he was full of enthusiasm, "Lorna, I really believe that we have at last cracked it, John Watton has just faxed me a revised agreement. It's not really what we were hoping for, but it is not as bad as the others. He is adamant, that this is his final negotiation, and he is not prepared to discuss conditions any more. This is the best that he will offer. He more or less implied that you could take it or leave it, so now it is up to you."

Gary continued, "Will you be able to get over to Karen's office sometime today? Make arrangements with her, and when you have read the document through, contact me again, and let me know what you have decided to do."

"Right, thanks a lot, Gary, I'll get straight on to Karen, and I'll telephone you later this evening."

That afternoon my husband and I went to Karen's office in Cardiff. We had not actually met her before, but found her friendly and helpful. However, she pointed out to me, "Of course Lorna, you must realize that in the end it has to be your decision what we do—yours and yours alone. Gary and I can only advise you, but you have to decide what you want us to do."

Then Karen went on to say what Gary and others were now saying, "I'm sure that if you stick it out, they will pay you the lot. I also have to tell you that if they won't, and you push them too hard, they are liable to take you for every penny that you have got. As you know they have a vast amount of money, and will do it through the courts. Let's face it they have nothing to lose. What is a couple of hundred thousand to them?"

"I know, and yet they will not willingly even pay me this small amount. But I suppose despite all that I will have to tentatively say yes to this last offer. I can't afford to lose anymore, I haven't got it."

"I know, and I'm really sorry, but I had to put you in the picture. Now, if you will sign here," Karen said pointing to the faxed deed, "I'll get it off to John Watton today."

When everything had been duly signed my husband and I went home and I telephoned Gary straight away.

"Gary, I've signed. I'm still not sure whether I have done the right thing, but it has to be settled one way or the other. Having said that, I'm appalled by the conditions that they have again attached to the agreement. I cannot honestly believe that they would stand up in court, but at the moment I am not going to argue. Maybe I will have a chance to do that another time. I have just about run out of steam at the moment, and don't feel as if I can battle with them any more"

"Lorna, don't give in now, we are nearly there, even though it is much less than you should get. Look at it like this. Half a loaf is better than no loaf at all or in this case a third of a loaf."

It helped that Gary could be optimistic, but I could not bring myself to believe that the deal would finally go through.

I received the revised deed through the post two days later. I read it and reread it, but nothing had changed and this was it.

This DEED is made the 24th day of May 1995 BETWEEN.
MRS. LORNA RICHARDS McBRIDE   Address.
CENTRON MANAGEMENT LTD   Address. (Centron)
Whereas Mrs. McBride has issued proceedings in the Cardiff District Registry of the High Court against Mr. Ivica Kalebic (Mr. Kalebic) under the court proceedings number and has obtained Judgment (the judgment) dated 21st. May 1991 against him.

WHEREBY IT IS AGREED AS FOLLOWS:

1. In the consideration of the sum of £25,000 (twenty five thousand pounds) to be paid by Centron to Mrs. McBride in installment specified in clause 2. Mrs. McBride as beneficial owner hereby assigns absolutely to Centron the full benefit and right and entitlement to the judgment, together with all and other rights, sums or benefits to which she is entitled, whether directly or indirectly by way of indemnity or otherwise, from Mr. Kalebic by reason of the claims

and matters pleaded by Mrs. McBride in the said proceedings (the claims).

2. CENTRON shall pay Mrs. McBride £20,000 upon the signing of this agreement by means of a solicitor's client account cheque, and £5000, on the 30th September.1995. In a like manner unless as at 30th September 1995, Mrs. McBride shall be in breach of this agreement, when such sums shall be held by Mrs. McBride's solicitors Richard Miller, Solicitors as stakeholders.

3.Mrs. McBride acknowledges and declares that by reason of this deed, and the assignment thereunder, she has no further claims whatsoever against Mr. Kalebic howsoever arising.

4. It is mutually agreed and declared by the parties hereto that these presents are confidential, and each party agree to keep the same confidential save for disclosure to their respective Legal advisors and to Triton Business Services (address)

5. Mrs. McBride undertakes that she will not personally or through any representative or agent, contact or attempt to contact Mr. Kalebic or any of his business associates or otherwise whosoever, or Mr. Kalebic's family or personal associates, save that this does not include any contact made with Mr. Kalebic's associates, which are of a personal nature to Mrs. McBride, and not concerning Mr. Kalebic.

Mrs. McBride further undertakes that in the event of any such associate inquiring as to the subject matter of this agreement. She will confirm that the matter has been settled, but not otherwise.

Mrs. McBride undertakes further that she will not directly or indirectly give any publicity in any matter howsoever, to all or any past dealing transactions or matters which have occurred between Mrs. McBride and/or her daughter Trudy McBride, and Mr. Kalebic or to the subject matter of this agreement.

Was all this necessary? Surely not. Could all this legal jargon be meant to confuse the issue? I am convinced that even the most astute would find most of it quite irrelevant.

Would it not have been easier for everyone concerned, if they had just said to me, "If you accept our offer YOU ARE GAGGED."

During the past months, particularly when I thought that I might at least get something, a celebration of some sort would surely be appropriate. Friends would ask, "How are things going. Any chance of that party you always promised when and if you got your money?"

"It could be possible soon, but don't bank on it," I'd say.

Now I realized that I was being restricted from doing even that.

Chapter 14

The first payment duly arrived after several hitches. It was paid directly into my bank, much to the surprise of the manager who asked me politely, when I went in to see him, "Might I ask who paid you this money, Mrs. McBride?"

"I wish that I could tell you, but I really haven't got a clue."

He looked at me very strangely. I wasn't surprised. I would have felt exactly as he did, I'm sure.

"I am sorry but all that I am able to tell you is that it is a long and complicated story of a debt that has taken me seven years to get this part payment, and one of the conditions in the agreement states categorically that I should not know who has paid me. I don't know why but there it is. I may find out one day, if I live long enough."

I continued, "Incidentally I want this money put into an account in my maiden name. As he is such a devious sod—sorry, but he really is. I want to make sure that he will not be able to con me again."

"Right, I will arrange that for you Mrs. McBride. Should you like any help about investing any of it, I can easily arrange for someone to visit you."

"Thank you very much, but I have not the slightest intention of investing it. After having waited so long, I am going to try and enjoy some of it while I can."

"I quite understand, but should you change your mind, don't hesitate to let me know, and we will help you all we can."

I am sure that they would as long as I had any money. In fairness, I have to say that this was a different bank from the one that had given me an ultimatum and no consideration at all, several years before.

Now, I had to wait another six months for the promised £5,000, and still wondered whether they would pay me or, would they find some excuse for not doing so.

As the whole affair had been made so public since the stories in the newspapers were published, it was difficult for me and my family once the matter had been settled.

Naturally, friends and colleagues, who had supported me, were anxious to know the outcome.

It became more difficult for them to believe that I could not really tell them.

They would come up to me with great enthusiasm and say, "What is the latest, have you had any of your money yet, and when are we going to celebrate?"

"I feel dreadful about it, but I can't tell you. They have restricted what I can say," I told them.

"Why, we've all been looking forward to celebrating. Haven't you had the money he owes you yet?"

"All I am allowed to say is that the matter has been settled, (to their satisfaction). They have made all the conditions for part payment and had I not agreed I would not have got a penny."

"So where do you think he got hold of the money to pay you?"

"He didn't, that at least I can tell you."

"Then who did?"

"I don't know."

"Come on you surely can tell me, you know that I have supported you all the way."

"I know that you have, and you know how much I have appreciated all the help that you have given me, but believe me, I really do not know who gave me this part payment. It was done through the solicitor who made all the conditions, one of which was that I did not need to know the name of the person who supplied the money."

"It sounds totally unbelievable, and if I didn't know you better, I'd think that you were making it all up," said my friend.

"Believe me, I'm not. Sometimes I wish I really was."

The enquiries went on for months, endlessly. We tried hard to avoid any discussion about the whole affair, and eventually for some unknown reason, at least to me, people stopped enquiring. Maybe they just became disinterested. The saga had probably gone on too long, and I was no longer news.

I must mention that I did have several phone calls from magazines and newspaper journalists, asking again if they could have the story to print. I was even offered payment.

I gave them all the same answer, "I am sorry that at the moment I am not in the position to give you an answer, and certainly no information. If you are genuinely interested, contact me after the 30th of September."

Nobody did. Although they had been most courteous while they had been speaking to me on the telephone, I came to the conclusion that it must have been someone from 'the other side,' who was checking whether I was prepared to breach any part of the agreement.

Midway through September, as I had received no communication from any party, I telephoned Karen to enquire whether she had heard anything.

"I was going to telephone you soon, Lorna, but thought that I would wait until nearer the 30th. I'll contact you as soon as I have any news," she said.

The letter from her duly arrived as promised, and it read:

Dear Mrs. McBride,
Re Ivica Kalebic.
I refer to our telephone conversation on 11th September 1995, and I enclose agreement.
I will be sending you a cheque of £5,000 with interest at the end of the month.

Despite all my doubts, the cheque arrived at the beginning of October 1995.

I had already paid my debts to the man, who had, through all his great efforts and to all the others without whose help I could never have carried on, I just had to say thank you with a celebration bottle. No party.

If you have read this far, I would like to say at this point, that without the hard work and dogged persistence of the man who I had picked at random from a previous newspaper story, I would never have got back a penny.

I keep remembering what Ivica said in the presence of solicitors and colleagues in an anti room after the oral examination. It will stay with me for a long time.

"IF I MAKE A MILLION, SHE'LL NOT GET A PENNY."

He might, or might not have made a MILLION. I have not heard any news of him since the last settlement was made.

Ivica was wrong about me not making A PENNY but then maybe he does not know.

I cannot understand why any one would be prepared to pay off a debt for someone else and want it to be kept a secret. Can you?

At the end of the last letter I had from Karen, she wrote, "I trust this is the end of the matter."

I'm sure we all do.

But for me I'm afraid, it never can be.

Chapter 15

I had decided to put the whole episode behind me. Although I would hope that one day my grandson would meet his father. He would keep on saying to me, "Please Granny, send emails to my daddy and ask him to get in touch, please." Naturally I did this for the child repeatedly, still no birthday cards or congratulations for his achievements.

Then quite unexpectedly, I received an airmail letter. Not expecting any contact from abroad at that time, I was more than interested. It was not signed but I knew immediately who had sent it, but could not understand why.

Of course it was from Pehin Isa's daughter, Mariam, who had married Ivica almost 20 years before. I was told that she had left him several years before, wanting a divorce and suing him for assault etc.

Naturally, as she was the niece of the Sultan of Brunei and the daughter of Pehin Isa, it made it no easier to try to get in touch with her. I was advised not to try to do so but I wanted to thank her for her apologies which I felt were genuine.

This is what Mariam wrote:

Dear Mrs. McBride,

Now that you have been made aware that your grandson has for some time been in contact with his father, I hope that you will at last enjoy peace of mind.

Please do not allow Ivica to make you feel at all or partially responsible for the way things were. It was always his intention to make you feel that you were to blame for him not contacting Alexander. There was no piece of paper that you made him sign with regard to Alexander. The only paper he signed was an acknowledgement of his debt to you, which he signed very reluctantly, on a visit to Cardiff to visit Alexander—it may have been at a cafe/restaurant of a hotel. He claimed at the time that he was not allowed to see Alexander, and only after he had signed was he allowed.

Ivica did not want you to be aware that he was in contact with Alexander because it was always his intention to "Punish" you, and he seemed to enjoy it when you would beg for him to contact Alexander. He would say with glee, "Let them suffer."

He said many awful things about you and your daughter which I am sure were undeserved and untrue. However, that is now in the past and we should all just let go, learn from these experiences, and move forward. Anyway he should not be allowed to continue manipulating you or your thoughts into blaming yourself.

Something I would like to point out to you, although this is not the purpose of this letter that neither I nor my family tried to discourage Ivica from maintaining contact with Alexander. In fact, I always encouraged him to do so, but his overriding mission was to torment you by making you believe that it was your fault for the breakdown in communication.

I hope that this has helped you in understanding the situation and that this will bring closure to this matter.

I wish you peace and serenity.

Of course Mariam's letter brought the complete reverse, so I tried to contact her.

Some time passed with no success. Again, promises came from people who said that they were prepared to help me if I paid for the information. Naturally this I refused to do. History seemed to be repeating itself. My persistent enquiries had obviously reached the Brunei High Commission in London, and, one of their officials rang my home and said that he might be able to help me.

Apparently a friend, who was an official in an embassy in another country, had a daughter who was a close friend of Mariam Isa. Of course, he said that he would need to get permission first.

"What is your name?" he asked.

Not wanting to get too involved I gave my maiden name. He rang back and said that he was sorry that he was unable to help me as Mariam had not recognized my name. After some consideration I decided to be truthful and was able to write a thank you which was the beginning of a regular email correspondence with Mariam and a visit from her to my home in this country. But of course this was the beginning of another four year saga.

The official from the embassy contacted me several times and kindly invited us to dinner with him in London. Owing to our advanced ages we unfortunately had to decline his kind offer. He also regretted having believed Ivica and told me that he was involved in Ivica's conversion to Islam, and that he had also written the translation of Ivica's wedding speech as Ivica had little knowledge of the language to be able to write it himself.

Now he was full of regret for having done this as most of what he had been asked to translate were lies and he was still ashamed of having helped a liar and a conman.

Of course, now that I was in close contact with Ivica's estranged wife, Mariam, Ivica became obsessed, and I received abusive phone calls and emails.

One example: This telephone call lasted about thirty-five minutes and consisted of total abuse most of the time. I was a wicked old woman who had stopped him seeing Alexander. Ivica said I rang Mariam every day. He said that Mariam is a lunatic, bought her degree, and can't even draw a straight line. He said that Mariam stops him from seeing Idris, their youngest son.

So I said, "Why will he not give her the divorce she wants?"

He literally screamed, "That's none of your business, Alexander is my son and has nothing to do with you."

Apparently Ivica was speaking from Bangkok.

"You have Mariam to your home. What on earth do you have in common? How can you even talk to her?"

Then Ivica shouted, and shouted, "Leave me alone you wicked old woman. Ask Alex to show you what Idris writes to me on Facebook. What have I ever done wrong to you? You want me dead or something? Alex and I love each other, maybe so, but I am afraid that you will influence him against his mother who looked after him for the twenty years that you did not because you—you wicked old woman, stopped me—and Mariam stopped me. Get on the phone to her now. She and her parents said that I should have nothing to do with Alex as he had a mad grandmother who was causing endless trouble in the Brunei embassy and the courts for no reason."

I responded that he knew the reason; it was that I was trying to get repaid on his accumulated debt to me of £64,000.

His abuse became obscene and he shouted, "Stop interfering and stop contacting that lunatic—now I'm telling you stop NOW or else. Her parents hate you."

I again told him of the debt that his father's-in-law solicitors acting for him had eventually repaid me less than half the debt out of which I was liable for high legal fees, so virtually was left with very little, having had to sell a property to pay off his original debt to a bank.

"You are a wicked lying old woman who upset Mariam's parents by trying to contact them to get my money back."

I was by this time very upset when he threatened me, "I'm telling you to stop being in contact with that lunatic or else—I'm warning you."

I put down the phone feeling very disturbed.

As usual, Ivica told his son that I was the liar—again, and unfortunately his son believed him.

Although Mariam has always insisted that her parents were not in any way involved, that is probably something I will never know.

Remembering what the man at the embassy had told me—that Pehin Isa had made full enquiries about his future son-in-law before he would allow

Mariam to marry Ivica and then insisted that Ivica and Mariam return to Brunei, leaving all business connections in this country behind.

Surely during his meticulous enquiries Pehin Isa must have learned all about Ivica's past and that he was a conman and a liar, but also a charmer as I unfortunately learned to my cost twenty years later.

My grandson, Alexander, went to his father for a holiday in Brunei. Needless to say his father completely charmed him and totally lied his way out of neglecting him for all those years and he came home and told me that his father had insisted that I have no further contact with his wife or else!

For the next few years, my grandson and I had a rather difficult relationship, sadly with many upsets. He, of course, was always making excuses for his father. His father's association with porn, illicit dealings etc. Now my main concern was that his father could well encourage Alexander into his way of life.

I followed with interest the cases concerning his father's divorce and assault with Mariam. It became a high profile front page story because of her relationship to the Sultan and being the daughter of Pehin Isa.

Imagine my surprise when a month ago I had a telephone call from my daughter, Trudy, "Mum I have a visitor here who would like to come to see you."

"Who is it?"

"Ivica."

My reaction was to say, "You must be joking!"

"No really, Alexander wants him to come."

What could I say? "Well, if you come with them, but please don't expect a normal welcome."

You can imagine how the next fifteen minutes dragged on until they arrived.

Ivica was his usual self. What he wanted me to do was to forget the past and to stop contacting his wife for his son's sake.

Again he repeated, "Why would you want to be friends with her; you have absolutely nothing in common and believe me she is only using you."

"How?" I asked him, "She is very wealthy, unlike me, there is nothing that I can give to her, so why?"

"She wants your friendship. You are her only friend, because everyone knows what a liar she is. Even her parents support me against her. All her family supports me. Does that not tell you anything?"

Eventually, I decided that I had heard enough, and said, "I have listened to all that you have said and I will think about it for Alexander's sake although I wonder why it is now that you appear to be so concerned about the same lad who you had refused to contact for all those years."

Ivica then unexpectedly looked at his mobile telephone for a number, wrote it down and said, "Ring this number; he is a great friend who will vouch for me."

When Ivica left, I did—another foolish mistake which I'm sure will never be resolved. I explained in an email to this friend what Ivica had said.

Ivica's "friend," a certain Mr. Vincent, replied that he had been employed in videoing and photographing a museum in Brunei that Mariam was designing for his client, Prince Jefri, the Sultan's brother. Half way through the project, his contract was terminated owing to the fact that Prince Jefri had urgent money problems elsewhere.

Mariam told him that she would be unable to pay him the £100,000 she owed him for the work that he had already done, because she had not been paid by Prince Jefri. Of course, Ivica insisted that she had and told me that he had been with her when she had been paid.

Mr. Vincent and I exchanged several emails and he said how sorry he felt that he couldn't help me as he had heard both sides of the story, and at this time was not prepared to speculate as to who was telling the truth.

I could not understand why Ivica would want me to contact a man who would not support him rightly or wrongly! I should not really be surprised as there have been so many inexplicable occasions during the past 20 or more years that I still cannot understand.

Now I feel I will have to stop trying. Truth, as they say, is stranger than fiction. How can we know who is telling the truth? Plausible liars appear so sincere but are so dangerous.

A few weeks later Mariam contacted me to tell me that the divorce had been granted in the Shariah court and sent me a copy of the notice that she had put in the Brunei newspapers.

In addition, I read the whole story on the internet:

PUBLIC NOTICE After nearly seven years of living apart and separate from Adam Kalebic Bin Abdullah Ivica Kalebic, Croatian passport number 003867785:00676356:002434126, Brunei Green IC No:50-895598, he has finally on the 8th of April 2011 at 4-30pm pronounced the Talaq (Jatuh Talaq) in the presence of Siti Mariam Isa and two (2) competent witnesses, at the office of Messrs Hj Ibrahim Al-Haj & Co, (Advocates & solicitors) Unit 297, 1st floor Block Chanderawasih "B" Puteri Complex Mile 1, Jalan Tutong, Bander Seri Begawan, Brunei, Durussalam. The said Talaq has been reported to the Shariah Court and is awaiting registration. Henceforth, Siti Mariam Isa shall have no connection whatsoever with the said person and he shall have no authority to represent her in any transactions or dealings, personal, business, or otherwise.

Siti Mariam Isa,
30th.April 2011

PUBLIC NOTICE
Please be informed that Siti Mariam Isa has retired from the partnership of Fratini's Restaurant on the 8th March. 2011. Her 1/3

share in the business has been purchased by Awang Musa Hj Adnin, who is now the majority partner of Fratini's Restaurant.

The Brunei High Court Suit No.22.of 2008 brought by Mariam Isa against the other partners of Fratini's Restaurant, has also been settled for an undisclosed sum and a consent order dated 31st March 2011 has been duly entered against the other partners.

Henceforth, Siti Mariam Isa shall have no connection whatsoever with the partnership and the continuing partners, in particular Adam Kalebic Bin Abdullah Ivica Kalebic shall have no authority whatsoever to represent her in any transactions or dealings, personal, business, or otherwise.

Siti Mariam Isa wishes to extend her utmost gratitude to Mr. Francis Chiew, Mr. Sylvester Leong and Lt Col (retired) Harif Ibrahim for their patience, industry and tireless efforts in helping to achieve this settlement with speed and efficiency.

Siti Mariam Isa.
30th April 2011

Naturally Ivica was now acting as the injured party, telling his son that Mariam had taken all his money and left him with enormous debts.

Mariam told me that she had taken only that which was rightfully hers. She had insisted that, during their whole marriage, it was she who had supported them all, including private education for the children, their homes and any other properties or businesses, also saying that it was she and her parents who had set him up in business when they left London.

My grandson repeatedly said to me regarding Mariam, "Granny that woman, your friend, has made my dad almost penniless."

Yesterday, unexpectedly my grandson called to see us. Naturally, I love the child, now a grown man, who at birth was not expected to survive. I have watched him grow into a highly intelligent man. Still it is painful for me to see him supporting his father in every way.

I just listen—and I listen. Alexander told me that his father had come to London on the weekend for business and had traveled to Cardiff for the day to see him. Alexander had been told to tell me, not to trust Ivica's now ex-wife, as she is only using me, and now that her father, Pehin Isa, has a new job with very high influence in Brunei, for me to be very careful as she has no reason to want me as a friend.

I have emailed her since but have not had a reply which is very unusual. I feel there must be a good reason and hope, that like that man to whom she owes money to said, "I would be very disappointed if I had been used." He wrote that he had liked Mariam and had believed her but would be very unhappy if he found out that she was not telling the truth.

And why did Ivica wait about ten years to tell him this? I can only assume why, and, really, at this point, it will make no difference what I think.

In 2011, with Ivica's current assault defense case, who knows what the outcome will be. And whether or when he will be taken to court to answer the "hit and run charge" against him. Well maybe I will never know.

All I can hope is that, whatever my grandson achieves in his life, it will not be NOTORIETY like his father, who all those years ago, said to his solicitor in my presence, "IF I MAKE A MILLION SHE'LL NOT GET A PENNY."

I am sure that this is the truth, which was seldom spoken by Ivica, unless it was for his benefit alone.

So maybe now I will be granted the serenity to accept the things I cannot change and the courage to change the things I can, and the wisdom to know the difference.

So be it!

CPSIA information can be obtained at www.ICGtesting.com
Printed in the USA
BVOW05s1036040914

365498BV00004B/312/P